IMPACT@WORK
Volume 3
Communicate &
Lead With
Power &
Presence

Speaking of impact:

There is only one way to avoid criticism:

Do nothing

Say nothing

And be nothing

Aristotle

From disucssion with readers:

Presence is a panacea

Impact arises from your ability to tell a good story – better than those people around you

Bobby Mehdwan

Bobby's had a 25-year career in blue-chip corporate management, coaching individuals and implementing change projects in perhaps a hundred companies in several industries all over the world.

He's seen the best of the best do what they are excellent at on countless production floors, office floors, in office networks and in boardrooms. In the process, he's won and lost many corporate battles and learnt many strategies on exactly what creates impact in the workplace.

Around the middle of his career, Bobby decided to make *impact* a big part of his personal development, wanting to know if there was a way to codify and replicate what the best of the best do naturally in order to elevate impact. Over the years, he found snippets and bit-parts of disconnected learning, but couldn't find a single place where it all came together. So, he made it his challenge to piece together one simple, all-encompassing system for everything he needed to know.

Through observation, systematic learning and practice, and by teaching others he's pulled together impact strategies you can use to significant effect.

Bobby's also a Master of Science and Bachelor of Engineering.

Cover by one designs

Published by 60 Strategies Ltd

You may also be interested in the Impact@Work podcast via iTunes or RSS

Find out more about other titles, coaching, training or speaking at 60strategies.com.

Connect

@bobbymehdwan   uk.linkedin.com/in/bobbymehdwan   facebook.com/60strategies

Contents

Introduction and About the Series

First of all, you've probably already covered this introduction if you've read another volume in this series. If that's the case, just take a look at the *Four Components of Impact* below to review the content of this book, then feel free to skip straight to the first strategy further on. These are numbered to precede or continue either side of the other volumes, with 5 dozen straddling the series.

Let's start with an idea – is there anyone out there who doesn't want to make a big impact? Anyone at all?

I think it's fair to assume we all want impact. In fact, we intuitively understand that it's something we all need in order to get ahead.

You probably know and want to emulate people with impact. You may describe them as having a natural flair, which seems to confer them an unfair advantage – unfair in the sense that we've introduced something that's about more than how hard they work, or how good they are at what they do. People with impact overcome obstacles with ease and engage others with grace, exerting influence on everything around them.

But their advantage seems as intangible as charisma.

Now, let's switch to – perhaps – your side of the table.

However hard you work, it can seem like others around you make a bigger impact *and* make it look easy. You have difficult interactions at work where you just can't get through to the people who are important to you – you see things one way and they see it another. You may have felt disadvantaged at some point in your career, as if you just didn't cut it and the feeling may have lingered like a chip on the shoulder – even if, on paper, you had the best accolades for your job. Others, with flair got promoted quicker, leaving you – working hard! You didn't enjoy or get the most out of what you were doing.

It's easy to label this as a confidence problem or consign it to feelings of inferiority in highly competitive workplaces. But if that is the case, what should you do?

Understand that there is limited value in simply trading self-work for recognition in the workplace. Churning out hard work is a hygiene factor (an expected minimum) in the most demanding of workplaces.

Learning to navigate the politics of an organization and understand how people work are more rewarding than *hard* work for more *hard* work.

Supremely impactful people practice impact strategies and thrive.

Impact means you're not just doing your own thing (which is easy) but doing it *with others,* which is much, much harder.

You can only stand out when you master working with others. But first, you have to master being worked with – making it productive and worthwhile for others to work with you. That comes from knowing yourself so you can put your best foot forward.

Mastering interactions may also be the key to enjoying your work. When you reflect, you may discover that you enjoyed, most, the work you did with people who clicked. The opposite is probably just as true.

Knowing yourself isn't the same thing as specialized technical knowledge about your chosen field. That's clearly essential to function effectively and fulfill your role – just as medics must know medicine and managers must know their business. Marketers won't get far without commerciality and so on. But what makes one marketer more impactful than another? Why do some managers make it up the pole faster, all other things being equal? It's not just their technical knowledge, but how they deploy themselves – in a deeply personal sense.

The big challenge for most of us is underinvesting in impact skills while favoring technical skills which look good on a resume. Those however are easily replicated and often abundant. They may confer diminished competitive advantage alone. Furthermore, in many industries, technical knowledge is merely a resource or perhaps a political currency if you know how to acquire and deploy it well, where others are involved.

Nevertheless, from this point on, we'll assume that you have the requisite technical skill, capability or knowledge for your role, because without that, little in this series will elevate you further.

So, What is Impact?

When most people think about impact, they visualize another person dressed to kill, communicating smoothly and powerfully, exuding magnetism and invisibly influencing others around them. Everyone's mesmerized, they turn to jellies and eventually melt into puddles!

Okay, so while the last part's a bit far-fetched, ultimately yes, this sounds like impact. However, this is projection (or delivery) impact and that's just one element of the whole package. Here's the thing – impact sits on top of a solid foundation. Without a foundation it's just fluff and blows around in the wind like in a cardboard TV character.

However, impact is also hard to describe. So, how can we tie it down?

Four Components of Impact

What is it that impactful people do? Are they born naturals?

That's certainly what I've always believed. And perhaps the answer is yes, by virtue of personality. But, it's almost certain that everything they know was learnt at some point, whether or not they were consciously aware of it – or even care to admit it.

If you practice impact, however, you'll be in rarified company that's difficult for rivals to replicate.

Technical skills and knowledge aside, some traits shared by impactful people are:

1. High levels of self-awareness and an ability to negotiate through challenging circumstances
2. An ability to focus on areas of strength utilizing tailored systems and processes to achieve goals
3. Confidence to project powerfully and influence others for the best outcomes
4. Highly strategic, competing vigorously when required and able to ward off rivals effortlessly.

In Volume 1: *Connecting: Self-awareness Behavior & Motivation* we saw how getting others to act for you is the very foundation of impact. We learnt what moves people – including you – and how your behavior elicits or hinders action. We understood how to stay the course so that you and others could make a positive impact in difficult situations. Self-awareness gave you some of the essentials of presence.

In Volume 2: Doing: Achieve Notable Goals, you learnt to do what you do best and do it the best you can. We turned your motivations from Volume 1 into notable goals, so you could create unbeatable substance with solid foundations.

Now, let's take a more detailed look at this book: *Projecting: Communicate & Lead with Power & Presence.*

This book will show you how to lead and face the world in a compelling way by telling good stories that get others on-side. We'll dissect leadership, story-telling and negotiation.

Impactful people project powerfully to influence others and situations for the best outcome. They:

- **Practice well-honed power-projection techniques in public**
- **Know how to communicate or negotiate to get what they want in every situation**
- **Use story and PR approaches to get people on board with their ideas and take others with them**
- **Lead others towards their own success.**

This book is what most people think about when they think of impact – because that's its most visible component. But that can be likened to the tip of an iceberg because projecting is supported by effective *doing (Volume 2)* which normally remains out of sight and below the waterline.

Can you project impact without doing much? Possibly, to the unsuspecting, but smart people will find you out quickly. You don't want that to happen when impact really matters.

I'll go so far as to say that *every* opportunity for making an impact that *ever* comes your way will arise from your ability to tell a good story, better than those around you.

When you move on to Volume 4: *Competing: Secure your Limelight* we'll look at how to stack systems in your favor and prevent others encroaching and stealing your limelight, which you created in the first three Volumes in the series. You'll learn how to leapfrog and carefully manage out rivals looking for a share of your spoils.

That's impact!

Four Components of Impact

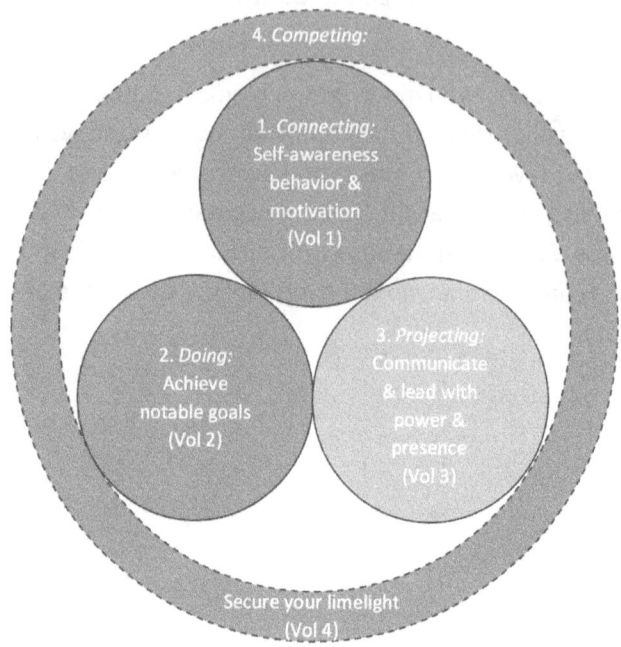

But wait a moment! You're up against a lot here!

Impact is clearly a skill set in its own right, just like knowing how to play an instrument or code a program or develop products. When practiced over a lifetime, it will push and keep you streets ahead of the pack.

Without any of these strategies under your belt, you're going to work every day without speaking the language of elites. If you think simply turning up, or doing what you do best, or training to improve skills, or putting in the hours, or doing what your boss wants, is enough to make a big impact, you're probably in for a big surprise. No matter what your capability or competence at your job, you *will be* limited and manipulated by others who know how to make a bigger personal impact. With most or all of the following strategies in your toolkit, you will be a powerhouse in virtually any organization or marketplace.

If you think that you're not in this game, yet you are going to work with other people, you *are* in this game. You're being played without accepting it.

How to Start

Several people I've coached over the years have said: *If only I knew this when I started...*

I couldn't agree more. In a sense, the series is written for my – relatively naïve – twenty something self, starting the world of work, clutching degree certificates and feeling like they meant everything.

Have you ever thought: *Wouldn't it be awesome if I could start again with all that I now know?* Well, start today.

I'll bet that one or two strategies make a big impression on you right off the bat. Go with them – you are adaptable to circumstance and not a slave to preference. Like coaching, read one per day or week say on your daily commute – then set your priorities on your daily agenda (I wrote the conversation styles in my notebook and left that page open during meetings). Ask a coach (or anyone) to observe you in action and provide feedback. That'll make the tips and tricks easy to digest and practical to implement. Repeat until they become habitual.

Stick with a strategy anywhere from a month to six, until it becomes automatic and feels normal.

In this series, I'll use myriad examples from the consumer tech, the arts (particularly story-telling) and other industries to illustrate the strategies outlined in each volume. Nevertheless, some will make immediate sense while others will come into play when you move on up.

Self-awareness alone will begin an internal change process that will show on the outside almost immediately – within days.

The series tries to move you quickly into *doing*, because that's vastly more important than simply reading, cogitating, or feeling motivated. I'll give you the *so what?* straight and easy, with real life lessons from some of the toughest work situations.

You'll find a key, which may help you prioritize the strategies:

Easy!	**Easy to understand with immediate impact!**
Persist	**Persist and remain alert. It will deliver!**

If this is the first time you've seen this material, it might hurt your head in places as you grapple. Persist and learn more about something that may not resonate at first.

Even if you find something familiar, just re-read it, because reminders are helpful when heads are frantic and memories fade. Consistency and persistence are key.

Now, have a journal handy – it's really important to try the questions if you really want to get the most out of this.

Take your time: remember that *presence* is a panacea. Presence builds resilience when combined with an understanding of your *emotional center* and – as you read in Volume 2 – mutually exclusive *options.*

Phew! Now try the exercise below. Look at the following diagram and try to figure out which inner box is a darker shade of grey.

Our Reality is our Perception[1] And Context is King –
Which Inner Box is a Lighter Shade of Grey – Left or
Right? (answer in the footnote)[2]

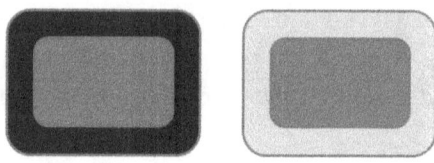

Did you get the puzzle?

No two people experience the world in the same way and our priorities, life position and context are all different.

To someone who has everything, everything else looks like opportunity. Conversely, to someone who's simply trying to survive, the exact same things can look like loss prevention. Your context is vital and a strategy may or may not make sense, depending on your life position.

---

[1] New research suggests that perception actually hides reality from us - but that's a whole different science! For now, accept that *our* reality is *our* perception (though perhaps not the *real thing*).

[2] Both inner boxes are the same shade of grey, though the context (outside shades) are different. Nevertheless, you see them differently. Our brains understand anything only by virtue of anything's relationship to anything else and not in absolute terms. Reality looks different to each of us.

Themes

You'll probably notice an underlying theme or two which may surprise you.

Firstly, being impactful requires you to challenge yourself and others – constantly seeking out the best way to do things, rather than just accepting the way things are. This can result in a lot of saying *no* and feeling contrarian.

Consider a statement from the late Steve Jobs, founder and vaunted ex-CEO of Apple and perhaps the most celebrated business leader in modern times: 'What I chose *not* to do was just as important to me as what I *did* do.' Now there's someone with impact!

Paradoxically, his sentiment is of increasing importance for all of us compared to even just half a century back. We now live in a distraction economy which presents us with excessive choice (partly the fault of Steve Jobs, in my view). A lot arrived with the internet, and it's now in our pockets on our smartphones. Every time we're in the company of others and turn to notifications from distant corners of the world, we relinquish easy opportunities to make an impact on those around us. However big or small, these moments add up. Notifications immediately throw us out of presence and when we act like this continuously, we go through a lot of our lives on our own islands with pretend connections. The benefit of saying no will often be freedom to be impactful in our own unique ways where it really counts.

Secondly, you may at first find the strategies make you feel self-centered, or even manipulative in some cases. That's a perfectly normal, but it's not the aim at all. You'll be finding your own voice.

You will also undoubtedly come across some unpalatable truths, particularly when we talk about getting the right things done in Volumes 3 and 4; but also throughout, as we unpack bias and influence. Fear not!

Questions

Before diving in, think now about what impact means to you and what you most want to work on. This will help you to home in on your priorities.

1.   What does impact mean to me? ....

2.   What do I want to work most on? ....

3.   Who could support or help me? ....

Projecting: Communicate & Lead with Power & Presence

Projecting is what most people think about when they think about impact.

But, what is projecting? Some people call it gravitas while others call it charisma or even charm.

Projecting powerfully is all of these, and when done well, it gives you an advantage that's virtually impossible to replicate.

Quite simply, you can't make an impact if you go unnoticed. Brains will filter you out as pedestrian if you represent no change to the norm.

You have to be notable for something – call it an x-factor – which can't be replicated easily to project well.

I'll also go so far as to say that *every* opportunity that *ever* comes your way will arise from your ability to tell a better story than those around you.

A couple of things to note, though.

You can of course start here with the impact series if you want, but do work your way through Volume 1 to find out what is fundamental about making you, you and others, themselves.

That will help you reveal your uniqueness when projecting and also help you understand how to get through to people using their own motivations. Many of the strategies in this book are explained with the help of what we understood Volume 1.

Also, impact – as a whole – is about creating a lasting impression, even long after you've left the scene. We're not just focusing on how you look or sound in the moment.

Big impact is not only PR and looking the part, but also substance beneath the style.

You cannot escape the need for a solid and sustainable footing. We cover that in Volume 2. Volume 3 – this book – prepares you for the PR and attention-grabbing game so you can stand out.

Beware – the biggest issue with a highly polished act is giving the impression it's all about you, and not the recipient.

You'll read later that that's the antithesis of trust. You'll need to reach beyond the polish, to a place where a facade isn't all important. It's a place where a bit of polish and an equivalent dose of humility and presence make all the difference.

Questions

Before diving in, think about the following questions and keep them in the back of your mind as you work through the training.

1. What story do *you* tell? ....

2. What do others re-tell of you (if anything)? ....

3. Do you tend to get your expected outcomes in negotiations?

....

Strategy #40[3]: Push and Pull Energy Redirection

Projecting is about wanting to be heard, wanting to be seen and respected.

Think of projecting in terms of *push* and *pull* – either pushing messages out or drawing others in like a magnet.

What you're really doing when you're pushing and pulling is aiming to *connect* with others.

It helps to think of energy re-direction when trying to make a connection. Drawing energy in is like coaxing it *from others*, whereas pushing it out is like *showering others* in yours.

Most of the time you're in the middle somewhere, doing a rapid-fire sequence of both in and out.

The trick is to pick the most appropriate energy re-direction for the situation.

It may help to visualize your energy hanging in the air like a magnetic field – or better still, like a halo that you can re-direct at will.

---

[3] Continuation from strategies 18-39 in Volume 2

Projecting with energy redirection

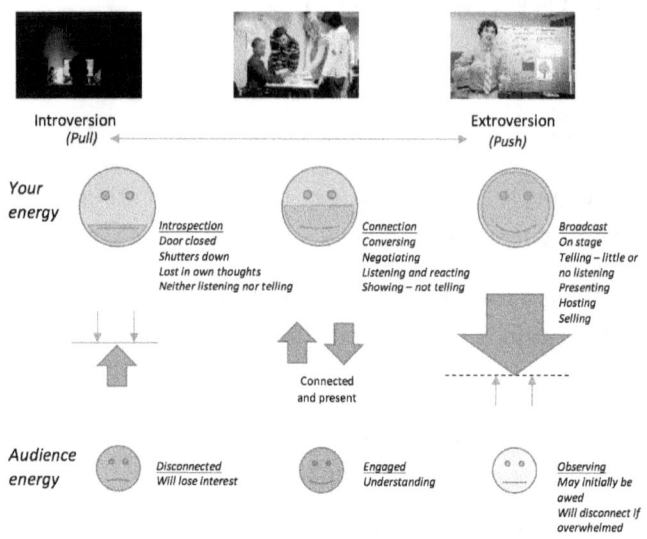

You probably have a good idea where you and others commonly sit on this scale.

Your norm will loosely correlate with introversion and extroversion; and I say loosely, because we can override our natural preference in different roles. Actors don't necessarily act when they're at home.

The commonest mistake when projecting is getting lost in your own thoughts when you're supposed to be 'on stage'.

Typically, people spend too much time mulling over their own thoughts in meetings, in social groups, in presentations and so on. The audience, expecting energy, receives little or none. That's the behavior on the left of the chart above.

And excessive smartphone usage can exacerbate this this unhelpful habitual behavior. While projecting well is all about looking up, the paradox is that we're now all looking down, retreated into four-inch screens in the name of communication, even when surrounded by others.[4]

Equally at the other end of the spectrum, some people seem to feel perpetually on stage, hosing down bewildered others with their words. Often these types fail to recognize when it's not their show and go so far as to encroach on some audiences without realizing. The broadcaster usually appears self-centered and lacking self- and social-awareness.

The trick, then, is to recognize what is called for in any given situation. Impactful people choose an appropriate style quite deliberately for different settings.

Remember that mind reading is for Hollywood aliens and broadcasting is for radio masts. Humans, on the other hand, have to communicate. Which are you?

---

[4] The irony is that having come out of a technology-led era of great vision in the 20th century, it seems that rose gold and a slightly better camera are now our commonest expressions of ingenuity and humanity's potential.

For introverts:

- You're frequently pensive, reflective or analytical in meetings and conversation, and your preferred state is probably introversion.

  But recognize that meetings and conversations aren't havens of introspection – they're stages and places for connection, respectively.

  Try to intentionally re-direct mental and vocal energy outwards towards your audience and less on your inner thoughts during meetings and conversations.

  Try to speak for at least a third of a conversation and listen or think for no more than two thirds.

- Recognize, also, that fairness is somewhat pitched against you. You don't need a PhD research budget to understand that extroverts are perceived as more valuable by the people around them. We're intrinsically biased to believe *what's focal is important* – it's called the spotlight effect or focusing illusion, and extroverts simply get more of the spotlight (you're also under its spell every time you watch or consume news or any specific media frequently).

Further, we we're wired to believe that what's focal is causal and that's a slam dunk for extroverted visionaries. There's no way around this, short of rewiring every brain on earth. Extraverted people also represent movement, which gets our attention, and what gets our attention is presumed important.

- When you are on stage giving a presentation or a performance, for instance, remember that this isn't the place for introspection.

    Stop doing it all inside your head, and focus on getting your energy straight to the eyes and ears of your audience.

    Move along the scale towards broadcast and imagine showering your audience in energy (so bring plenty)!

- If you're normally introspective, be aware that you may come across as closed. Others may feel an invisible barrier and feel disconnected.

    Worse still, they may come to feel you sucking them dry of energy, especially if they bring it each time!

    Failing to overcome the mental barrier you put up, others will disengage, so introspection can be self-reinforcing.

- Nevertheless, introspecting is an appropriate energy state when thinking and working alone, or trying to avoid external distractions.

  This energy state's most appropriate for *Focusing and Getting It Done* in the productivity system in Volume 2. It can useful for implementing habits and routines too.

For extroverts:

- Broadcasting is an appropriate energy state during the diversity stage in our productivity system in Volume 2.

  It is most helpful when others need telling or you need to get your point across; but it should not to be confused with connecting, which is a two-way exchange.

- If you are the one doing all the talking in a conversation, recognize that that's *not* a conversation.

  If you want a conversation, don't put yourself on stage – your companion many not have come looking for a performance.

  Try to intentionally stop vocalizing the stream of consciousness unfolding in your head and re-direct your ears towards your audience's mouth.

Listen for two thirds of the time and *build only on what's said* for no more than one third.

- If you are on stage, or normally an extreme extrovert, you might feel that your audiences often lack energy; in that you get less back than you put out. This is a common illusion due to the imbalance.

  Your broadcasting triggers a habitual response of a watching mode in others, in which they would not normally mirror your energy. The show's going on inside their heads.

  If interaction is what you are seeking, you'll have to turn down the broadcast.

- **If you're constantly showering others in your point of view, you won't have a connection. They'll expect to move on, just like when a show finishes on television.**

Understand that neither introspection nor broadcasting are particularly present states of mind. In both states, you're always somewhere else mentally; you're either thinking of doing something, being somewhere, or telling someone about something else.

For connection:

Move to a more present state, by connecting to whomever is immediately in front of you.

- The centered state is called connection, in which energy flows in *both* directions. It's the appropriate position for daily interactions.

     This is the best style when negotiating what you want to focus on. We looked at this when we triaged incoming requests in Volume 2.

- Recognize, however, that others might want, or need, to work alone and not collaborate for some of the time. **Allow others to disconnect for appropriate periods.** Move to, and also allow movement to, the left of the scale above.
- **Others simply want to be told what you think sometimes.** Not every interaction is a conversation or a negotiation, so the stage is sometimes yours for the taking. Move, and allow for movement to, the right on the scale above.

     The strategies in the remainder of this book are grouped as 1) push and pull combined; 2) primarily push and 3) primarily pull.

Questions

1. Do you normally push or pull in communication? ....

2. How does that impact your connection to others? ....

3. What would you like to do more of? ....

4. When is a different style appropriate and how will you do it? ....

1. Push and Pull (Combined) Strategies

Strategy #41: Communicate & Negotiate Purposefully

Do you know how to be heard? Must you always shout from the rooftops?

Communicating is quite simply story-telling, and story-telling requires the attention of an audience. So, what hooks attention in a story? A challenge.

A challenge is something to *overcome*, and that makes it *purposeful*.

When you are purposeful, mirror neurons fire in the brains of your audience and they become attentive. Even your body language will say that it's time to pay attention whenever you are purposeful.

We'll dissect story telling in detail below, For now, how do you communicate with a purpose? First, understand what that purpose is.

What's the purpose of your communication?

Be Authoritative (Push)		Require (Push)	
1. Make a clear **suggestion** 2. Give **reasons and data** 3. Back up with useful **insight** 4. Then **listen & modify**		1. Express your **feelings** 2. State your **need** 3. Clarify any **rewards or Consequences**	
Connect (Pull)		Inspire or Persuade (Pull)	
1. **Summarize** what you heard 2. Then **listen and reflect** on what was said 3. **Explore or question** what was said		1. Express your **support for a cause** 2. Provide a supporting **personal disclosure** 3. State your **vision**	

Purpose in communication can be couched in terms of whether you want to push or pull.

You'll also notice how the first step in each style aims to get attention at the outset, then follows a specific order to structure your communication effectively and fire it home.

Good communicators flex their style, and use all quadrants where appropriate.

Let's look at them, one at a time.

Be Authoritative

You might use this style when *pushing out* a solution to a problem.

This style is best suited to writing – particularly business writing, reports and recommendations – but it can also be effective in meetings, when worded briefly.

You state your suggestion clearly and efficiently at the outset so the audience knows immediately what you're about. Avoid the tendency to write a narrative then state a conclusion. Turn it around, especially in emails.

You want to avoid misinterpretation and to stand tall over what you want.

That's a hallmark of authority, and appeals to Controllers, the de-facto operating mode of corporate management. We opened these up in Volume 1.

You'd then provide your reasons and suitable back-up data, which appeals to Analytical types. Next, provide any insight to support your position, stories or concrete examples and evidence (not opinions) if you have any and hammer your point home.

This insight can be a corroborating experience or some inside information and shows that you've covered your bases and have requisite experience. Insight is also hard to dismiss when it's relevant and appropriate.

Finally, because you may still be wrong or may still not have a good position, listen for feedback and modify your suggestions accordingly.

This demonstrates humility, openness and trust by virtue of lowering self-interest (we'll explore trust below). It also brings you back down the Ladder of Inference, which we looked at in Volume 1.

As you can see, you've also spoken directly to all the predominant operating modes in corporate settings.

This can be a good style to anchor a negotiation.

Require

You may choose this style when something just has to get done, perhaps on your terms.

You might use it to order or direct a team and even to *push* people around.

You start by revealing disappointment about a situation, because your feelings are hard for others to dismiss. They will subconsciously feel compelled to rescue your ill feelings.

You then clearly state what's required and to hammer it home, you make clear the rewards for compliance and the consequences for non-compliance.

This appeals to both positivity and negatively motivated individuals.

Connect

This is the language of *pull* in the sense that you're getting close to others and what they think.

This is not so much telling them what you think. You'll use this style in conversations to collaborate or to understand different perspectives to your own.

This is a good style with which to negotiate.

You begin by briefly summarizing what you understand of a situation. Express doubt in your perceptions if any – this shows humility and opens the door for openness. Then, to demonstrate listening and engagement, you listen and reflect on a response to your summary.

You must stop and understand how the information/view point that you're listening to moves your own point of view and also demonstrate active listening by helping your audience elaborate on what they're saying.

Ask relevant questions to explore and build upon what's being said.

Inspire or persuade

Let's say you want to inspire or motivate action for a vision, in a sense *pulling* others along.

You begin by offering your support and acknowledgement of a cause, or plight.

Here, you're validating the cause and encouraging everyone to recall their own support in their own minds.

You then disclose something personal and relevant to show authenticity.

The revelation might be a personal pain point or struggle aimed at demonstrating empathy – understanding the plight and building trust with your audience. You might even go so far to demonstrate that you yourself need your own medicine (for instance: a change that you're espousing) along with everyone else. You're trying to get buy-in for your story and be relatable.

Opening up like this is normally the hook of political leaders. In a sense, they're saying: we're all in this together. They're leading by example.

The logical outcome of that connection then is *the vision* itself.

This is the new state of affairs that negates the pain of the old world. When the audience has bought the plight, as painful as it may be, the vision is much harder to reject.

Don't be tempted to start with the vision and then explain.

If it's a big vision, the shutter might drop, at which point the listening stops. Done the other way round, you're actually getting people to focus on *their* plight, without them necessarily realizing it.

This can be a good style to break down an intransigent negotiation.

Here are some further strategies for purposeful communication:

- Be clear on what you want and be deliberate when using *push* communication

  This means thinking ahead and having clarity over what you want, how you will say it and pre-empting potential reactions.

  It's about anticipating what's likely to get in your way before launching in and also being clear about how you might overcome objections.

- Getting others to respond to email can sometimes feel like *pulling* teeth.

  How do *you* get the responses you want?

It may sound obvious, but it pays to keep emails short and *action* oriented. Try the 3-sentence rule, which is exactly what it says.

Have you ever noticed that the emails you read right away are the one-liners? And the ones which you save for later or ignore tend to require page scrolling or appear as dense text? Scrolling is disconnecting, especially on a mobile device.

In business writing, it's the norm to say what action you want up front, then explain if necessary; it's not like writing a novel.

If people have to comb or scroll for an action, assume that they won't. If they buy the action, they'll thank you for not dragging them through a lengthy exposition.

Ditch email and do it on a call. When you send email, you attract more email. To stop it, *you* have to stop it. I once worked with a manager who never replied to my email, so I eventually stopped sending them and we ended up talking a lot more for the better.

If you must send an email, which is even remotely contentious, **first write it and leave it as draft.** Then, imagine that it's really gone. What do you feel? Is it what you wanted? Are you prepared for the fallout? If not, change it.

For more strategies on managing email communication specifically (as a distraction), see Volume 2 on Triage.

Questions

1. Which styles of communication do you most use? ....

2. Which would you use more of for your role? ....

3. How will you prepare or remind yourself of what you've

   learnt here in the heat of battle? ....

Strategy #42: Tell or Collaborate?

We'll now look at the choice of communication styles where you want people to act on something, do something or adopt a change. It's vital to know how best to present your ideas in order to carry through a change or decision.

Choose the wrong communication approach and you'll leave your ideas open to challenge and fail to get the support you expect. At worst, your ideas will be derailed without you seeing the problems approaching.

It's necessary to understand the cycle of change when making decisions, because useful decisions that work always bring about a change to a status quo – be it big or small – and there's a common perception that people resist change. That's not entirely true in my experience.

Everyone's enthused by their own brand of change and desire to *improve the world* in some way. That, of course, surely means everyone else needs to change!

It's clear then that change is proposed, adopted or rejected (continuously) for self-interested reasons. The key is to involve others in decisions that are difficult to push through, the theory being that they will push with you. If you can get people behind you, there's simply a greater force working on your side.

Other times, it's best to break through resistance quickly, to avoid grumbling and delay tactics, or even sabotage. Others often also overcome the pain of change quickly if it's short lived.

Push or Pull? Imagine a Swing

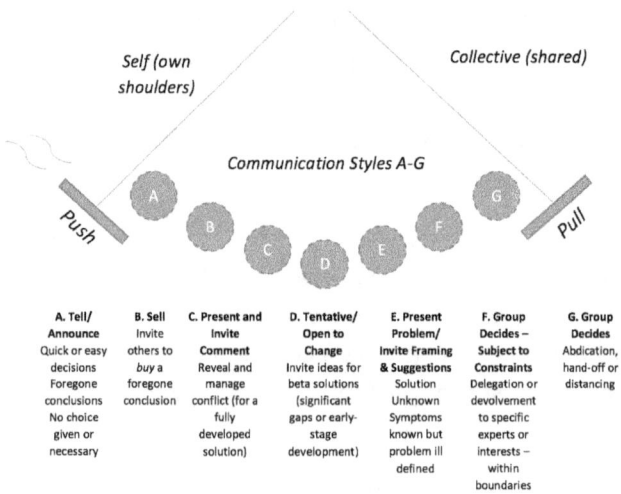

A. Tell/ Announce	B. Sell	C. Present and Invite	D. Tentative/ Open to Change	E. Present Problem/ Invite Framing & Suggestions	F. Group Decides – Subject to Constraints	G. Group Decides
Quick or easy decisions	Invite others to *buy a foregone conclusion*	Invite Comment Reveal and manage conflict (for a fully developed solution)	Invite ideas for beta solutions (significant gaps or early-stage development)	Solution Unknown Symptoms known but problem ill defined	Delegation or devolvement to specific experts or interests – within boundaries	Abdication, hand-off or distancing
Foregone conclusions No choice given or necessary						

Going from push to pull or A to G:

Tell/Announce and Sell (A & B)

Smaller decisions are often *announced*, as in A on the left side of the diagram.

These can be based on existing processes and rules and the approach works well in the absence of choice, leeway or time for discussion. The impact of what is communicated may be small and the solution obvious or even potentially lifesaving during dire circumstances.

The push end of the swing (A & B) can also come about after a long period of consultation or where negotiation isn't necessary or possible.

The audience feels informed but not included in what's communicated. They are essentially *told*.

A softer version of this approach is to **sell** a decision, as in B.

This, again, is without any real intention to relinquish authority over the solution.

But selling isn't involving. It's pretend telling.

This can be a good style to anchor a negotiation.

Present (C & D)

Managers often *present* well-formed solutions or decisions and invite comments.

Strictly speaking, these are foregone conclusions and comments are normally only invited to confirm support or to understand positions.

A softer version of presenting is to provide something as **tentative (D)**, with a call for input from a smaller group of people who may rely on an outcome or solution, or who are impacted by a change or decision.

This approach often comes during late-stage development of a lengthy consultation. Like telling, presenting is a good style to use at the completion of a consultation.

Being open to comment is more suited to the later stages in the completion of a project or consultation, allowing for final tweaks and adjustments.

This can also be a good style to establish a position in a negotiation.

Group decisions (E &F)

At the *pull* end of the swing, we get collaboration.

This approach is best where solutions to problems (or even the problem itself) are unknown and require consultation to flesh out.

It's suited to the early stages of consultation, or where others have superior knowledge.

The approach can be useful in communicating that a change is coming prior to any serious solution

building. This approach, however, is time consuming, expensive, slow, and vulnerable to sabotage.

Unless your overriding need is meritocracy, extremes at this end are best avoided. You could break large change initiatives into chunks and consult only where required.

Opening up in this way is usually the first step in a public consultation or for information gathering.

This is usually a good style to consummate a negotiation.

Abdication (G)

This is a useful approach where others are better able to make decisions, and where, for instance the impact on you will be negligible or nil – or you simply want nothing to do with it.

Questions

1. Which of the seven communication styles do you most often need? ....

2. Do you confuse telling and selling for involving? ....

3. Do you involve others when you'd be better off telling? ......

Strategy #43: Defensive versus Offensive

This strategy is as simple as it sounds.

When you're on the offensive, you'll come across as purposeful. In contrast, defensiveness *always* comes across as someone wanting to avoid responsibility.

Defensive

Counter-intuitively, this is the language of push, in the sense that you're pushing back on differing opinions – preferring to push out your own view or at least stand your ground.

Take for instance a performance review, where your manager tells you that your performance could have been stronger. When you're defensive, you're likely to find fault elsewhere or try and rationalize away the perception. Worse still, you might say that the issue *was someone else's problem,* or that it *relies on someone to do something else first.*

All of these statements say: I walk into problems and I don't take responsibility for what happens to me; I don't accept feedback and I can't figure things out when challenged.

In a real sense, you're *pushing* the situation or people away.

It's the antithesis of personal leadership and you're highly likely to befall this approach when defending a presentation or pitch which went wrong in public.

In these situations, it's *always* best to listen and acknowledge feedback first and foremost, whatever it may be.

Your main aim is to show maturity rather than indulging in the need to be right. Remembering that right is just a difference in opinion and a game of majority.

The desire to be right is born of self-interest, and as we'll see later, that's the inverse of trust.

But don't be too hard done by – majority (or right) is also another way of saying *average*, and is more a measure of effective marketing than anything else.

Offensive

You won't now be surprised to find that this is the language of *pull*, in the sense you're pulling others in your direction.

Offensive approaches, on the other hand, aren't offensive in the traditional sense. We're not angry, aggressive or swearing – those are ways of bullying and avoiding.

We may, however, be tough, persistent and even a little intimidating if necessary.

We're *pulling* the universe in our direction by showing understanding of a situation; we know what we want and have the connections to achieve it.

This is the language of leadership. Whatever the circumstance, *always* look like you're in control, even when you're not.

That doesn't mean being brash or dismissive, just know what's going on and what you want. The only variation is to show impatience for interruptions as a power act; you could say things like *let me finish* or *let's take this outside*, or override interruptions.

Pay attention to whenever you're on stage – research suggests that simply acting a part becomes self-fulfilling.

Questions

1. Do you adopt a defensive style under attack? ....

2. What would be the benefit of turning that to offensive? ....

3. Are you rude or dismissive when you want to be offensive?

4. How might you tone that down but still remain in control?

2. Pull Strategies

Strategy #44: Build Trust – and Power

What is trust?

It's not a warm fuzzy feeling – it's just an equation. I kid you not...

The trust equation! Scary how predicable we are

$$Trust = \frac{Credibility + Reliability + Intimacy}{Self\text{-}interest}$$

Your *credibility* is your reputation or capability, whereas *reliability* is your track record on delivering and finishing something you're committed to.

Intimacy is about openness, authenticity and empathy, whereas *self-interest* is the complete opposite – me, me, me!

Self-interest, therefore, is the antithesis of trust.

If you look at the equation, you'll see that it does in fact make intuitive sense. We'll talk more about it when we look at Competition in Volume 4.

To explore the equation a little further, let's look at the explosion of interest in home working and controlling your own time over the last decade or so[5]. While anyone can espouse the benefits of home working, I've increasingly found that young professionals need to understand the adverse impact that that style of working has on trust with colleagues.

Working alone reduces visibility and lowers intimacy, and whether or not you put in the expected graft at home, a loss of intimacy always means extra effort to evidence reliability. Working from home when there's a perfectly good office to go to will also give create a perception of self-interest, whether intended or not, however small it may be.

Put simply, you're more trustworthy if you're a known entity with an appropriate level of intimacy and visibility. We simply don't trust others we don't know well enough. You can't build currency if you're never around.

Trustworthiness also goes hand in hand with corporate ownership – if you're low on the trust scale, it's much easier for your boss to disown or fire you when the wrong time comes.

And the trust equation applies to organizations too. A good example of this is when I was at an embassy recently, to register a legal document. Credibility started low – the embassy website was unclear with

---

[5] This social movement is perhaps best encapsulated by the popular book *The Four Hour Work Week* by Tim Ferriss

hidden process requirements dotted around in different places on different pages. I *fully expected* to be sent away with administrative to-dos, which could have been resolved easily on site with the words 'your papers aren't in order'. The embassy then destroyed its own reliability – its website required a specific appointment time, with no leeway for lateness, though I then had to wait several hours to be seen! Intimacy was all but missing – all document processing was conducted behind barriers and instructions barked back through a glass wall. It all seemed to add up to self-interest – a process aimed at providing the Embassy with legal protection and conducted at their convenience, whereas the whole transaction was initiated for my purpose and didn't otherwise require the embassy's involvement. On a trust scale of 0-10, it was close to zero – and not just for me, but for the entire waiting room of a dozen or so anxious people with the same simple need. Furthermore, the interaction primed self-interest in every participant like an infection – it became easy for everyone to hyper-focus on their own needs before helping others to expedite the process for everyone.

So, now that you know how trust works, let's explore the individual variables a little more.

Credibility

Here's where you believe someone *can* live up to their words and act with integrity, whether they decide to or not. They have the power or position to act if they choose.

In your head, you ask, does this person make sense? Do they really understand what's going on? Do they over-simplify and demonstrate a lack of understanding? Do they make threats and commitments they can't carry out? Do they even look the part? Do they have the right technical expertise?

In professional circles, credibility usually equates to someone with capability, real world experience or the network of business contacts they claim to have.

When it comes to credibility then, actions and track records speak louder than words.

That's the single most important reason why *Volume 2: Doing* in this series is as crucial for impact as Volume 3, which you are reading now. Volume 2 is all about acting efficiently and effectively.

Longevity also counts for credibility. Moving into an area where you lack heritage and experience can invite dismissiveness from others. A lack of heritage can invoke strong Parent types to treat you as Child (see Parent Adult Child in Volume 1).

But, perhaps the biggest threat to credibility is over-promising and overselling.

Whenever you're listening to a pitch, perhaps given by a Promoter, look for evidence of delivery on commitments and fair representations.

Integrity counts here too. When something's on plan, hiding the truth threatens credibility, whereas appropriate openness – however uncomfortable – always conveys integrity and courage.

Finally, the most powerful way to *demonstrate* credibility is via *social proof*.

Simply put, this mean others in a powerful or independent position vouch for you. It's the central idea behind ratings in all walks of life, whether for products and services or performance reviews at work.

Credibility is vital in a negotiation.

Reliability

Reliability can also be called dependability. Does someone make promises they never keep? Or change course without warning? Do they have a track record of delivering late, or never? Whenever others follow through on commitments and also do what they say – consistently – you judge them to be reliable.

Promoters usually have the most work to do here. Common traits are not showing up and under-delivering – and usually without warning or foresight. When promoters can't deliver, they should try to give appropriate warning and agree new timetables early to keep a reign on expectations.

Reliability can be used as leverage in a negotiation.

Intimacy

Another word for intimacy is *openness*.

It's hard to trust someone who's closed, absent or hides their intentions or position. It's also difficult to trust someone who doesn't listen but only tells.

Intimacy can also be a willingness to take on a position of vulnerability. It allows, amongst other things, for others to see the pebble in your shoes just like the one in their own. It makes you human.

But it isn't an invitation to air your dirty laundry; it may simply be an acknowledgment that it exits!

Paradoxically, revealing your innermost concerns can be a show of confidence if done professionally.

If you've read Volume 1, you'll recall the TA Drivers. If you have a *Be Strong* driver (common in Controllers), you'll need to spend more on building intimacy in order to connect with others.

Intimacy can be used as leverage in a negotiation too. Use it to unstick an intransigent negotiation.

Self-interest

This best describes people lost in their own needs, views and in general self-concern, epitomized perhaps by the selfie generation.

The self-interested put themselves first in everything they do. They *tell* a lot, and they aren't *really* interested in the needs of others beyond easing conscience or boosting self-image. They want to be right – always.

Unlike credibility, reliability and intimacy, all of which you want to boost in order to build trust, self-Interest needs to be kept in check in you're to build trust.

Because self-interest is the inverse of trust.

Highly Controlling or Hurry Up types should slow down and loosen attachment to their wants, at least sufficiently enough to listen to and understand the needs of others. These types should be prepared to park their agendas, judgments and perspectives and learn to understand, but not tell. They should practice letting go of being *right* all the time in order to build trust.

Self-interest appears to be exacerbated by a threat of loss. It's as if our general loss aversion kicks in as a defensive reaction when credibility, status or position are challenged. It's heightened by scarcity but tends to abate with abundant resource and opportunity.

The message from the embassy example above is that you should remain aware of environments that trigger – and influencers that prime – your self-interest.

Unfortunately, self-interest also seems to have become the overriding social conditioning in Western society over the last half-century or so, perhaps as a result of increasing corporatization. In the context of the trust equation, it's not surprising that we now feel more disconnected than ever, despite the myriad of communication channels in our pockets (trade secret: they are marketing channels for the self-interested). When we look at the protagonists in business culture, story and the movies, we are almost uniformly presented with role models of self-interest. Only the best of the best turn outward in the end.

High self-interest kills a negotiation.

Untrustworthy

It's a safe bet to expect closed and analytical types to be less trustworthy in general – mainly because of our perceptions of intimacy and reliability, respectively. Analytical types simply calculate their way through life, changing course as per their answers and not necessarily on their commitments. This can be deemed unreliable or unpredictable in a general sense. In fact, being closed and calculating (analytical) may also be describe as passive-aggressive (we'll review this below) and we don't find that particularly trustworthy.

If this is you, you may have to compensate with increased effort on openness. If this means you're more introverted, you'll have to work harder on revealing your internal calculations.

Corporate life is highly analytical, and organizations are generally havens of self-interest, when highly competitive. Standing out – for trust – in such an environment, could just be your x-factor.

The Leadership Paradox

It's important now to understand how the trust equation can be expertly manipulated by power players. The reality is that leaders and managers, particularly, aren't engaged to deliver trust, per se – but instead to deliver results, or simply to move people to action where they'd otherwise fear to tread. Call it manipulation of trust for a greater good.

Genuine intimacy can be fatal to a leader whenever there's any room for self-doubt or otherwise – we all know that in corporate and political life at least, that means almost everywhere, and pretty much every day of the week.

So, does that means leaders, managers and politicians aren't trustworthy? In my view, you simply can't implicitly trust those roles if their aim is to lead or manage. A trustworthy leader or manager is unlikely to be effective. In all power plays, intimacy and truth are manufactured to feign control and a solid grip. Power players also work extra hard to conceal self-interest by accentuating specific elements of style during public displays. We'll review these when we discuss building rapport below.

What these managers, leaders and politicians are betting on – in the trust equation – is credibility in delivery, while trying hard not to sacrifice the other elements of trust. Unfortunately, this lack of freedom to be genuinely open, often means it's a lonely place at the top.

Spotting tall tales

As we've read above, we all conceal and lie – big and small – as a natural course of interaction. Small lies avoid unhelpful or unnecessary distraction, whereas big lies avoid fear of loss.

But what if you want to root out a fib? Test your suspicions with this approach:

- First, discuss a <u>known truth</u> and carefully observe body language. You're looking for openness (lips free of tension, natural eye contact, visible hands), sufficient details in description, speed of recall and so on. Make a mental note
- Second, discuss the issue that's being <u>concealed</u> and carefully observe body language again. Notice how it changes. You're looking for changes from

openness to closing down (pursed lips, searching eyes, looking or turning away, hidden hands, hands to face, leaning back, folded arms), hiding, frequent repetition in descriptions, rigidness, over-compensation (unnaturally still, staring eyes, jabbing fingers, qualifying statements). Ensure the teller isn't pre-occupied e.g. typing or reading email, as that'll complicate detection and suppress leakage!

- Third, finish with a <u>known truth</u> again and see if signs of tension ease
- Fourth, go test your trust if suspicious.

Questions

1. On a 1-5 scale, which element of the trust equation do you personify most? ....

2. How does that impact your trustworthiness in the eyes of others? ....

3. Which element do you need to work most on to generate more trust? ....

4. How will you remind yourself to do these things? ....

Strategy #45: Ask for Help

It's important to stand on your own feet to build credibility, but impact isn't necessarily about walking alone or Being Strong or Trying Hard (in the language of the TA Drivers from Volume 1).

If you remember the trust equation, you'll know that trust is built upon intimacy and that can mean asking for help and support.

So, it pays to ask for what you need at times. And it's so obvious that most of us don't do this. We overcomplicate things and take the long solitary road.

When you do this properly, it shows humanity and a desire to allow others to share the work – and its rewards.

When you ask others for help, they get the chance to feel smart and valuable – that's how leaders work. It's called flattery and others will often thank *you* for making them feel valued.

But don't be high maintenance or sloping shoulders. That's just self-interest again.

Questions

1. What are you trying to achieve that could *really* do with help, support or input? ....

2. How will you ask? ....

3. What's the return for the other side, or are you committed to repaying the favor some day? ....

Strategy #46: Generate Rapport and Power with Presence

We now know it's natural to like who we trust. A trusted quantity is familiar and familiarity neutralizes fear and the barrier of distrust.

Humans are uncomfortable with uncertainty. Politicians, for example, are impossible to vote for when they're unknown, whatever they prescribe for a nation.

The rapport-building strategies below turn you into a *known* likeable quantity. Their aim is to eliminate distractions, barriers and friction – such as uncertainty – which get in the way of your impact.

You can't build rapport or support when you are distant. You'll always be trumped by others who are more familiar.

And, if you want rapport or power, get in front of those who are important to you – frequently.

Building Rapport

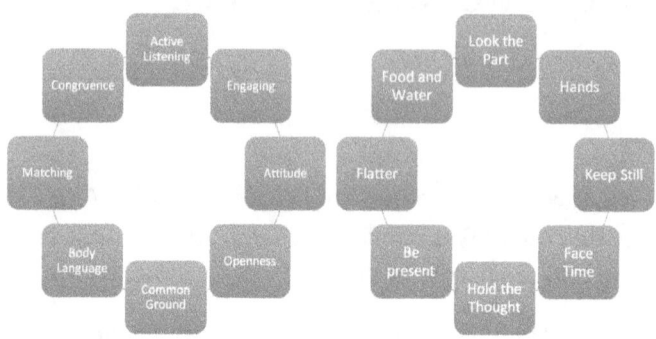

Here's what to do when you get face to face to build rapport.

Active Listening and questioning

Listening is the keyword.

If you do nothing else, learn to listen without judgment or your own opinions.

If you work in a bravado culture where you're compelled to contribute at all costs, you may well *feel* like a limp fish when you're listening.

But first recognize when you're *on stage*, and when you're *back stage*. You're on stage for instance in group meetings, workshops, interviews and presentations. You're back stage, for instance in one-to-one conversations, which have the advantage of intimacy to build trust.

Second, when you listen, *show* attentiveness – that's the *active* part of active listening. Probe and question in a way that *moves* the *teller's* perspective on. You might summarize to show you've understood.

Encourage the teller to bring *their* words *to life*. The active part, if done well, shows you've listened and accepted what was said without judgment or opinion. Use open questions to get dialogue e.g. How are you? Use closed questions to close it down e.g. Are you okay?

So, why does this build rapport? Just like you – and me – others like *nothing better* than to talk about themselves and their own opinions, all day, every day, even given just half a chance.

This turns listening into the easiest form of flattery, and it's welcomed no matter what the circumstance or language.

How do you know that you're listening well? Let's think about energy re-directions:

- When you're *telling*, all of your mental energy is projecting outwards. The signs are: interrupting, forcing your view, re-loading to speak next and speaking over others. When everyone's at it, you're part of a shouting match
- When you're *introspective*, all your energy is directed inward. The signs are: mumbling, having to repeat yourself, avoiding eye contact, feeling

ignored or dwelling on what was said earlier. You're almost immediately thrown into introspection when there's an uncomfortable silence in a conversation

- When you're *connected*, however, and actively listening, you're using two ears and one mouth in that proportion. This is a connected state, because, unlike the other two states, **ears and mouth, when used together, make a conversation**.

Engaging

One of the best ways to build rapport is to build upon the ideas of others during a discussion.

In contrast, a style of grilling and questioning without adding – or pointing out shortfalls – can be one of the biggest turnoffs imaginable.

It's always difficult to build, whereas any fool can question or undermine.

Supporting and encouraging someone to persist through challenges and unknowns can yield magic.

So how do you know that you're engaging enough? Let's think about the energy re-directions again.

- When you're *telling*, you're saying 'it's my way, or the highway!' This is an appropriate style when domination is key, say during a crisis where there's really no room for a negotiation. Strong management is called for

- If you're *introspecting*, you're keeping things close to your chest and not revealing good ideas or the potential issues. This can be deliberate passive-aggressiveness or simply a feeling that your ideas are not worthy, or that it's not your place to speak
- When you're *connected*, however, you're thinking 'let's combine ideas.' You're most likely to do this with colleagues, peers and underlings. Finding a subtle way to do this with seniors and managers will really put you on the map. By subtle, I mean anything that doesn't shatter or challenge their belief in their superiority (they will *never* thank you for that).

Attitude

Taking a genuine interest in other people will show for itself and convey flattery.

You're displaying good attitude if you're actively listening and engaging.

Openness

Revealing something *relevant* and intimate about yourself builds intimacy as we saw in the Trust Equation

Others will feel as though you're entrusting them with personal secrets or inviting them to a special place of trust – even if it's not actually the case.

Again, this is flattering to others, and people accept flattery without condition.

Find common ground

We've said before that people are trusted when they're a *known* quantity.

So, find common ground when you first meet someone.

Do they support the same sports team? Did they go to the same school? Do you have mutual acquaintances? What you'll find is that you'll instantly have a bond that no one else around you has – however minute and irrelevant to your shared connection is.

This is an easy unfair advantage to gain.

Speak body language

It's pretty well known that your body speaks louder than words. First impressions are almost entirely non-verbal – friend or foe, warm or cold.

Two thirds, or more, of what another person *hears* when you *talk*, is your body speaking. You really don't have a choice in the matter – it's simply how our brains are wired to interpret the world.

So, don't ignore the need to pitch your body along with your words or your well-crafted words will fall flat.

There's also mounting evidence that simply acting a part affects not just in how you feel, but your physiology too and how others perceive you. If you read Volume 1, you'll know that it's experience which leads to forming beliefs, and also that your subconscious can't tell reality from fantasy. Acting a part is therefore self-reinforcing.

Matching

This is also known as mirroring, and produces a subconscious feeling of cognitive ease in others – all without their conscious realization.

When you walk and talk with someone, match their step and stride (try alternating your stride and you'll feel the connection sever instantly).

Matching also works when sitting, for instance in a meeting. Scratch your nose when the speaker does, cross your legs in the same direction as the speaker and so on. All other things equal, your speaker will feel more connected to you.

Be Congruent

You can't profess to be interested and engaged while looking around for distractions.

Remember your body speaks louder than words. In terms of the trust equation, looking at your smartphone, for example, shows excessive self-interest which diminishes trust.

But being incongruent can help you as well. It's an ideal way to signal the end of a conversation, without having to say so if you've been attentive up to that point!

Look the part

Like it or not, we are distracted by style as a proxy for substance. Almost anyone can be dressed up for something they are not with relative ease. While looks may have been a valuable proxy in times of scarcity (most of our evolution), that's rarely the condition we find ourselves in today.

And we've said several times now – known quantities are more trustable. Looking the part turns you into a known quantity which matches the expectation of others.

But remember that brains process images – particularly faces – well before we are consciously aware and use then heuristics (stereotypes) to form instant impressions. This is because our brains are predictive in order to conserve energy.

Not looking the part, however, also becomes a known distraction which can get in the way of your agenda or conversation.

While looks aren't everything once a person knows you well, don't let scruffiness get in your way unnecessarily for the wrong reasons, especially when you need to form a good first impression or tackle something without distraction. Remember, familiarity produces cognitive ease.

Handy advice

People subconsciously dis-trust you when your hands are hidden from view.

We're wired that way to avoid danger – who knows what weapon you could be holding under the table or behind your back! Keep your hands on the table when you're in meetings and keep them out of pockets or folded arms when talking to someone.

Folded arms are a no-no as they put a mental barrier in the way for others and mentally re-direct your energy towards introspection.

Folded arms could reveal you're judging what you're hearing rather than accepting it openly for what it is.

Go one step further and touch someone for a better connection. It must be discrete and professional like a handshake or a tap on the shoulder.

Touching diffuses the subconscious urge to look for danger.

Keep still

When talking to an audience, do you like to walk up and down? Do you think it adds energy?

Well, how often do you see the President walking around giving a press briefing? Not at all.

The truth is that tracking you around a stage is extra work for an audience. It also suggests a lack of confidence whenever the movement is random and continuous like a nervous tick.

Mentally, moving around is like trying to escape your words – like saying them, but not standing for them.

If you need to demonstrate power, firmness and confidence, stand still and tall, right at the source of your words.

Moving also suggests that the speaker is lost in their own thoughts or introspecting. But remember what a stage is for. It's for projecting and connecting. When you want to connect in a conversation, do you walk around? No. So treat your presentations like a conversation with the people in the audience if you want to connect better.

Does it ever make sense to move? Possibly, if it supports the connection with the audience, for example, handing the audience something to look at, or speaking to an individual sat out there.

Hand gestures, facial movements and flexing of the body, e.g. leaning forward, can also subconsciously demonstrate power, emphasis, physical presence and confidence.

These gestures are somewhat like draping yourself over the space. It's a primeval domination tactic commonly used by animals, but it only works if you are genuinely, credibly able to carry it off.

Face Time

If you have a face, use it. A lack of visual expression is perfect for a recently plastered wall but fatal for your impact on others.

One of the worst things that can afflict you is teenage Botox face – where the lights are on but no one's home.

Use your face well. I see great faces wasted from disuse and a blank slate is the problem. Expression is the answer and requires interaction, which requires little more than presence in the company of others.

Remember, people mistrust others who are shifty eyed because, sub-consciously, they're trying to be invisible and avoiding openness. The eyes shift continuously between staring and looking away to relieve *their* discomfort. But they probably just don't know how to speak with their eyes. They could just *point and shoot* – but that's not great either.

Try looking and speaking in 3rds and noticing eye color to build rapport.

Imagine the eyes and mouth as an upside-down triangle, the mouth being the lowest corner. Simply go around the triangle 1-2-3, holding each corner for a second. A second each is ideal.

Remember that connecting is listening 2/3, and speaking 1/3.

Listen while gazing at the eyes because the eyes do most of the talking. Speak then, when your gaze drops to the mouth.

When you drop your gaze below eye level, for instance to the mouth, you appear open, but sometimes subservient. To appear dominant instead, just turn the triangle upside down so the high point is on the forehead.

Hold that thought

We all love to speak our mind given half an opportunity, but I suggest that you refrain from blurting your thoughts out when you meet someone – that's if you really want to be *heard*. With some people, it is better to wait for the right moment.

Just like you, everyone's distracted by their own thoughts. They arrive at meetings with unique perspectives and experiences.

Initially, therefore, they cannot often even hear what you're saying above the din inside their own heads.

Paradoxically, one of the best ways to be heard is to first listen. Start by parking your own agenda.

Allow others to get whatever they want off their chest first – this is particularly valuable with superiors. When you find the right opening, re-focus the meeting on your agenda. You'll be amazed at how open others become once they've cleared their heads. Why does this work?

More than anything, it demonstrates your respect for the views of others alongside your own. With superiors, it shows maturity, humility and deference and demonstrates wisdom when operating in hierarchies.

When you hear out superiors first, you get the lay of the land and you can tailor your words accordingly. They receive the respect they feel *entitled* to (and perhaps get to play Parent against Child which comes naturally to superiors with children).

So, having gotten their Gestalt, they tend to be more open to listening. All of that generates trust.

Remember, you'll appear confident – not clinging on for dear life to whatever it is you're after. When you do eventually start on your needs, reciprocity then kicks in – you've listened, and others then feel compelled and more willing to listen back.

Those of you with a strong Hurry Up TA driver (see Volume 1) can try this approach for better connections.

Be present

Many people comment that former President Bill Clinton is charismatic, pointing out his enormous *presence*. Having not met him, I can't vouch for that, but it seems that his presence generates huge rapport with whomever he meets. But what does *presence* actually mean?

When someone's present, they're not just there in body but also in spirit and mind.

They're not pre-occupied by their thoughts, distractions or desires to be elsewhere. They're not thinking about others while only half-listening or ignoring the person right in front of them.

You can take a huge step towards presence by actively parking your thoughts and banishing distractions (including smartphones) from meetings and conversations.

Give yourself no choice but to connect fully with the person in front of you for however long or short feels right.

Often, however, putting physical distractions aside isn't enough. Our own thoughts can be our biggest enemy particularly when a mental loop keeps playing inside our heads. That pulls us out of presence and intimacy in a moment.

Imagine putting your thoughts in an imaginary box as you enter a conversation or a room.

The imaginary box could be in the corner, or on a table, or just outside the room. Picture yourself putting your thoughts inside and closing the lid, knowing that they'll still be there when you're done. You may have to repeat this several times if distracting thoughts keep popping up but over time you'll train your brain to act in the way you want. You may well also find that you rarely, if ever, pull your thoughts back out of the box again. Ask yourself then is cogitating just a useless distraction? Probably, you may conclude.

My failsafe, go-to trigger for presence is *a decision* to focus on others around me and *park myself* for a moment.

The conflict to be present or elsewhere immediately lifts a cloud. It moves me from introspection to listener, then back to connection, the temporary reprieve forced on the brain allowing me to step back and find a new perspective. It gives time for the pressure needle to drop. I find yourself more objective and clear when I return to my thoughts later.

Create and practice the triggers that push you back into a present state whenever you feel flustered, frustrated, wired or unsettled. Practice these triggers and schedule time with them frequently. They could be music, sounds (chirping birds), a phrase (mine is: you get more of what you focus on), sitting or standing quietly (I use that trigger to choose how to spend my time more effectively), your Eisenhower matrix (from Volume 2), your children, photos of family, talking to someone – anything.

But presence has a lot more to offer than important moments of connection.

Presence is a panacea for distracted brains.

It has the power to kick the world in the ass and your troubles out your door when you don't need them. It's your free breathing space at the worst of times, neutralizing pain, grief, anxiety, want, ego and attachment, fluff, bluster, doubt, illusion, delusion, hope, loss, regret, envy, jealousy, rationalizing, willpower, vision and whatever lurks outside the door – whether in an imagined future or stuck in the past.

When you're in the vacuum of uncertainty, when there's no lamppost or solid familiar ground to stand on, practice presence.

If frees you to make the most of the moment and it's as real and as tangible as real gets. It doesn't ask for faith, hope, salvation, redemption or even a wallet. The only thing that remains is your foot on a pedal in front of you. That's incredibly liberating!

We often refer to young children as charismatic. What we're actually taking about is that, by virtue of their inability to think of future or past burdens or responsibilities, they simply remain present in every moment.

Flatter well

Flattery always works. Always. Period.

It can even be disingenuous – but that matters not a jot.

Flattery is instant gratification and likability on a plate.

Why? Because it's nearly impossible to reject well-crafted, or even poorly pitched flattery.

It can be delivered in words, via a smile or a laugh and even on a large trowel, simply to show that you're enjoying someone's company or conversation – even if you're not.

Girls: allow the guys to tell the jokes and always giggle. Pretend, if you have to.

Food and water (or coffee)

Sustenance instantly distracts us from malaise – whatever it may be – reminding us how great it *feels* to disconnect from the dog-eat-dog world outside the window and simply be congenial over a coffee or lunch.

It can also help solve a genuine energy deficiency and works to a greater or lesser extent without fail every time, eliciting reciprocity when offered.

Project power

Several of the strategies above are essential for
projecting power.

**Fundamentally, power projection is little more
than a well-polished act, utilizing specific techniques
consciously and deliberately.**

The key power projection tactics are:

- Standing still and square on, *on stage* (anywhere
  public)
- Open, welcoming hand gestures in public
- Draping yourself over space
- Economy with words and speaking deliberately with
  lowered voice pitch
- Dominating style eye contact (inverted apex)
- Arriving last at meetings (meetings)
- Creating audiences (meetings again)
- Doing the talking – and reprimanding interruptions
  (meetings again)!
- Looking the part (meetings – help)!
- Humor
- Presence
- Last, but not least, bravado and hubris. Feigning
  control and concealing doubt are non-negotiable
  when pitching vision and making speeches – you
  can read more about this in the Leadership Paradox
  under the Trust Equation.

Realize that these projection tactics are self-reinforcing. Remember, neither you nor your audiences' subconscious can tell fantasy from reality – unless your projection is over the top and totally unbelievable or inappropriate.

So, power players must generate meetings to remind us who's boss! Look out for these in a power play near you.

Questions

1. Which of the building-rapport techniques do I most need to work on? ....

2. What's the benefit of doing them – or consequence of not? ....

3. Where, when and how will I do them? ....

4. How will I trigger or remember the behavior I want? ....

5. What will I work on next? ....

Strategy #47: Work the Charisma Formula

Many of the strategies we've already discussed in Volumes 1, 2 and 3 will help you to boost your charisma.

But what exactly is charisma? Well, for a start, it's surprisingly formulaic and not particularly mystical.

Charismatic people don't *need* to give a shit – but *do so* proudly anyway! Charisma is a life position.

Charismatics have a loose grip on life, always seem to have options up their sleeve and arrive with bags of presence.

Here are some other characteristics you may recognize. They:

- Have superior wit and social grace. These emerge from of intense presence
- Are funny. Humor makes *anyone* instantly likeable. Why? A good joke reveals common ground and reminds us all that life is still okay – whatever adversity surrounds us. The keys to getting a laugh are:

- o Surprising irony – which appears like a flash.
  Avoid mocking or denigrating unless everyone is
  certain to share your perspective
  - o Restraint. Not laughing at your own joke –
    immediately – reinforces surprise and irony
  - o Timing. That's the flash
  - o Experience and insight. You have to have
    experienced life's ironies to reveal them
  - o Humility, if you don't get the laugh. You're
    essentially offering yourself up

You can see how spotting ironies relies on a high
degree of presence.

- Have a *unique* way of packaging and looking at life.
  They don't necessarily go with the crowd
- Bring enough energy to pull everyone else along
- Have self-control, but are also mildly insensitive.
  Charismatics are happily disagreeable at times, but
  this is offset by charm at other times. I usually think
  of former President George W Bush – both revered
  and reviled in equal measure – and this dichotomy
  is itself a good indicator of charisma. The villains in
  our stories are usually the most charismatic
- Have confidence to show their authenticity
  (genuine or not), whatever their style
- Are congruent in physical appearance and
  demeanor. Scruffiness and indifference may serve
  to accentuate what's already truly great about them
- Remain present, when not in their own tree. They
  willingly step out of their ivory tower to simply be
  with you, now. This is presence

- Are scarce, but for a genuine purpose. This is known as the *hero's journey* in fiction. They must have a tall tree to climb, which suggests some important endeavor or value at stake. It is their strong purpose which permits indifference when they are absent. After all, the President would be part of the furniture if he were as visible as the weather girl.

So, what is not charisma? Absence or indifference for whatever's in front of you, now.

Day to day, this is signaled by checking smartphones in meetings and looking for distractions from conversations. These together, when they become the norm, convey self-interest (the inverse of trust).

When people are introspective *on stage* and lose control over time (general busyness), they are avoiding responsibility for their relationships. That's not charisma.

Question

> 1. Which of these characteristics could you spend more time
>
> developing? ....

Strategy #48: Master Conflict with a Yes, Instead of a No

You get conflict whenever you put people into an arena like an office.

It's part of the territory, because offices create new things and new things mean change.

We're also continuously negotiating for what we want and need – every minute of every interaction.

Change and negotiation bring conflict.

Others resist change and many need pulling along, kicking and screaming in many cases, if they must come along.

So, conflict results in a lot of saying *no*, out loud or under your breath.

But conflict doesn't just come about with change. There's competition at work and that necessarily means you're up against competing aims. Everyone wants as big a share as possible of a fixed money pot, be it an employer's coffers, sales to customers, the size of a market etc. Each of us, business or individual, tries – every day of our lives – to redirect as much of that finite spending power in our direction. Spending power, however, is a scarce resource and you'll be disagreeing continuously with everyone else who are also trying to pull it their own direction.

Saying no to what you *don't* want is an essential life and work skill. Get good at it, because differences in opinion, experience, perspectives, wants, needs, demands, ego and so on make-up 95% of office interaction. When you put any group of people together, anywhere, and for any purpose, you'll see continuous conflict to a greater or lesser extent.

It's fundamentally human to have differing agendas and hierarchies which pull resource in their own direction.

Yet, many people have huge problems with saying no, even to whatever might be considered inappropriate treatment. Saying no feels like we're fueling the conflict we wish to avoid, and it goes against our innate compulsion to reciprocate and be civil to others. There's a lot working against no.

But, while co-operation is certainly a force for good, saying no – effectively – when warranted, can be much better for all concerned.

Saying no *is* necessary in order to get the best out of ourselves and others, particularly in a world that throws hundreds of new distractions in our direction each day.

How can we possibly sift out the *very best* if we can't say no to the average majority? Most of us simply end up living diluted.

How can we say no effectively? First, remember that *no is in fact just a really good yes.*

No should *always* be accompanied by a yes for something preferable – always.

Yes and no are simply tradeoffs between various options and not absolutes in themselves. When you say no to something *good* you're freeing yourself to say yes to something *great.*

No isn't a rejection, though it can feel that way. It's a *choice* to do something that's different to whatever's simply put top of mind.

When *we* experience rejection, because of a no, all we're really facing are differing points of view and differing agendas – mine versus yours. Neither is right nor wrong – just different.

My view comes from my experience, goals, position, expectations, aims and so on – and yours, from yours. They are rarely, if ever, the same, so don't expect that.

In a conflicted relationship, mentally step forward in time and ask: do I want it to work in a year's time, or to the win the fight now. What would a friend advise me to do? Get out of your head and see it objectively.

Now, try these steps to invoke an easier *no:*

1. **Process.** In a difficult negotiation, discuss the process first before getting into the specifics. It makes people less defensive and closed.
2. **Tradeoff.** Imagine that your boss says he would like you to do X – but, for whatever reason, you don't want to. In a disagreement, you might focus on the tradeoff between your time and whatever it is that deserves a yes. When done carefully, you can, in most circumstances totally avoid the using the word no. It will simply emerge as a theme without the word being said
3. **Persist.** Now, persist when you say no. Most people relent quickly in the face of conflict, believing that conflict is a bad show. But it helps to see conflict as a means to an end, which is separate from you. A popular phrase enshrines this is as 'the *problem* is the problem – *you're* not the problem'
4. **Graceful exit.** Third, conjure up an easy graceful exit from the conflict for others. You'll find that many people prefer an exit to stem the anxiety of conflict. When you do this well, they may not even realize they've been set up to leave the game of *their own* volition
5. **Presence.** Fourth, remain as mentally *present* as possible in the face of conflict. Though it's natural to project negative outcomes, it's also self-defeating. Playing that loop over and over inside your head is terminal and serves only to kill resolve. It's a story which only guides you back to the safety of the cave. Remaining present means that you've detached yourself from the outcome emotionally – whatever it may be

6. **Stay open to options** assuming they've stayed the course, don't be disrespectful, challenge the issue, not the person. Don't assume you have the whole picture. In fact, ask for advice, even if it's for something tangential (this lowers defenses). If, from this point on, you continue to challenge, recognize that you're in a power struggle. If you get into a fight, stop and recognize how you might just be fueling it.

7. **Agreement.** Consummate something which keeps the focus on what the conflict is about, otherwise you'll walk away feeling it was about you

8. **Prepare to be reviled...** Eventually, you'll have to get over being liked. Remember, that you're at work not to be liked per se, but to achieve something noteworthy and better – that means change, and change means conflict within a status quo (wherever you see status quo, you rarely see the noteworthy). Remember we said that charisma is equal parts revered and reviled?

    Though it's good to be liked (we've talked about that a lot in this series), it's better to be feared for the good of something greater than your own needs. To make this work and enhance your credibility, you really must pitch your needs in a way that negates any notions of self-interest on your part.

9. **...but don't cross the boss.** Finally, never throw rocks at your boss or their perception of themselves. It just doesn't work. Boss just means my opinion counts more than yours round here.

Just like you, they're simply not wired to appreciate challenges to authority however right you might feel. Position someone else to do it for you if it's truly necessary to get a message through.

But, what if you have to challenge a boss? What do you have to know? First, recognize that disagreeing with a superior conjures an unhealthy fear of implications because you are inherently negatively biased and losses loom large in your brain. Start by expressing your boss's point of view and lay some common ground on the table to ensure she feels acknowledged. Then, build your case and support remembering it has to have some grounds and that 'right' is just a game of majority. State your intention to disagree before you do so and focus on the facts of a disagreement, not your opinion (a boss' opinion always trumps yours so don't simply walk into that arena). Express humility, like: I'm thinking aloud here, be open to alternatives and create a safety zone or the defenses will come out (loss aversion again, which inhibits the frontal cortex and engages the more emotional fight or flight parts automatically).

Though conflict sounds like an all-round problem, my advice to managers is to encourage at least some conflict within your teams. You can do this by inviting constructive challenge and competition for good ideas. If nothing else, you will be preventing others from getting lost up their own ladder of inference[6], by stress testing their ideas.

---

[6] We covered the Ladder of Inference in Volume 1

Questions

1. To what do you need to say *no*? ....

2. What something, that's greater, gets the *yes*? ....

3. How will you use the technique of saying *no* to deliver it

   with grace? ....

Strategy #49: Leaders Help Others Achieve *Their* Success

A lot's said about leadership, and there are as many perspectives on leadership as there are self-styled leaders.

Beware, being at the top doesn't signal a leader – there's a huge distinction between leadership and management. A leader can also manage, but a manager isn't a leader.

Limbs all sound like the same thing, but arms and legs can't be confused for each other and so it is with leaders and managers. You may have noticed that I've rarely – if ever – mentioned leaders in the series and that's to keep things in perspective.

For the most part, business requires doers and managers, not leaders. Using the language of Operating Modes from Volume 1, managers are *Controllers* or *Caretakers* and use analytics to quantify and tell others that things are either on track, or not, and what to do next. This comprises the vast majority of senior corporate roles in status-quo businesses. The instant a management function can be replaced by Artificial Intelligence, it will be.

Leadership, however, is the operating mode of promoting and supporting – with controlling and analysing still there, though in the background. I don't think we'd ever willingly acquiesce to being led by code in a box, or a hologram, so leadership as a role is here to stay.

There's a big difference between managing spreadsheet or key-click producers and channelling the motivation and energy of people for change or a new path.

Leaders emerge, whereas managers are provided with a title. Leaders take responsibility for the success of a collective by utilizing all the resource available. Managers rely on and are propped up by the collective, rules, processes and reports.

If you want to be a leader, just remember one simple principle:

Leaders help others achieve their success.

So, what does that mean?

It means that leaders achieve impact *last*. They succeed *after* their people, not before. Their impact is bestowed *by their people*.

Think of Martin Luther, Mother Theresa, Gandhi, Moses and so. Yes, lofty examples, I know, but the point is that none of these were given to the world, waving the title of Chief Saviour or Director of Heavenly Affairs – or anything else, demanding respect. Each of these emerged from the norm, to first identify then fill a vacuum.

But a leader also isn't simply operating on the whim of the people. By virtue of position or role, they have the power or authority to remove obstacles and keep their people moving through their *own* challenges.

But how do you know when you're leading well?

If you simply live the one leadership principle above, you'll be on the right track. You won't need an MBA, title or accolades to prop you up.

But a good sign is whether you feel in sync with your led, despite obstacles and differences. And you can only be in sync when you are present.

But why does all this work to *elevate* a leader?

Leaders thrive on reciprocity. You see, real leaders never ask for permission to lead. They simply emerge. Think of the leaders in your life.

A team confers leadership to the person who rises to the challenge and fills a void.

Leaders, fundamentally, are a projection of their followers' own wishes. A group's desire embodied, they cherish the idea that the leader represents. She simply emerges when a group votes to crystallise its own aspirations. He is the individual who best confirms, validates, channels and reinforces the group's pre-existing desires. In fact, the group sees to it. And in the most extreme of circumstances, leaders are simply wishful thinking of their followers, granted. Think of history's great political leaders. Even Hitler. As soon as the idea goes, the leader tumbles with it.

Conversely, leaders who are instead given their positions are creations called managers. But managers don't represent the group – they represent...management.

More practically, as a leader you'll need to rally clarity[7], direction, resource, knowledge, focus, motivation, coaching, facilitation and promotion of ideas.

The best leaders require courage and mild insensitivity.

They utilise positive motivation, but are equally adept at leveraging negative motivation – call it carrot and stick. That's because *everyone* needs cajoling at times. *Everyone.* Humans are inept at getting the best out of themselves. Why? Well, we're up against the competence cycle and loss aversion[8]. We simply don't see or are dismissive of our own blind spots and it takes the courage of a leader to save us from our self-imposed limitations.

But that can be hard for leaders, for we all cling dearly to our safety nets. Being fearful is built into human DNA. Moreover, leaders don't control – they usually herd cats. It takes proactive effort to lead.

---

[7] Conversely, ambiguity is a useful competitive weapon. More on that in Volume 4.

[8] Loss Aversion and the Competence Cycle are covered in Volumes 1 and 2 of the series respectively

Leader must also be adept at managing uncertainty, because there are never instruction manuals for leaders need to go. And this is the most essential condition for leadership to emerge. Can you tolerate it? Proactively tackle it? Provide clarity in the darkness.

Leaders, above all, bet on the actions of people they don't directly control, but can only influence. Living with that is much harder than either doing your own thing by yourself or *telling* others to follow the rules (read: managers).

Leaders sometimes receive recognition, but many times they don't. When they keep it about others, they always find *impact* – though their personal impact is secondary.

So, my advice is to just lead wherever you lead – you don't need permission.

Give your energy to your domain and you will signal that something is worth caring about. You will set the bar on effort, commitment and the results expected. Stand square and drape yourself over a space that's undeniably yours. If enough people want it, you'll get the lead.

Finally, you can help yourself by learning to get commitment from others. Try publicising examples of required performance and creating singular enemies or challenges to bring disparate people together – that's how wars are won. Your people will then have a model of behavior and fulfil it of their own volition.

Leaders never get aggressive, bullying, arrogant or prideful or even demanding, because that, instead, is called micro-managing. It's a different role.

So, we all like to call ourselves leaders, because it sounds grand, though that's not our role at work. For the most part, it's to manage or man the treadmill.

For more on leadership, review the techniques on building rapport and the trust equation above.

Questions

1. Are you happier managing or leading? ....

2. What would you be able to lead at the drop of a hat? ....

3. If you manage a team, how could you lead more? ....

Strategy #50: Create Bandwagons

Impact and success come packaged as bandwagons. And bandwagons are *made* – not *purchased* in a store.

Real impact, however, is what you can make from what you have at hand. Or, even better, what can others do with what you've created.

To return to the tech industry for an example, Steve Jobs, former CEO of Apple, created bandwagons as often as he created i-devices. As a result, a multitude of new industries now survive and thrive off of the Apple products which he and his team dreamt up. That's his real impact.

Harry Potter and *Star Wars* are bandwagons too. All sorts of big interests continue to prop up the characters, mainly because they make big bucks doing so.

The trick for big impact is to use your energy to create a bandwagon that everyone can jump on. In the words of leadership, that means your success comes second.

You're after a stream of work – a stream of income – that others can support and help you maintain while taking a fair share of the spoils.

How do you create a bandwagon? Creativity, marketing and leadership are king. You can read about how to be creative in Volume 2.

Strategy #51: Deliver Bad News in a Shit Sandwich

Bandwagons are great, but they can be derailing too. That's bad news in most corporate spheres, where it's impossible to shake-off a run of bad luck.

In Volume 1, we looked at confirming ideas and the Ladder of Inference. Once someone's associated with adversity, those ideas cement quickly and are difficult to shake off, even in the face of evidence that disproves your beliefs. This evidence will be readily ignored, discounted, or distrusted, so we can all continue to act in a manner consistent with our beliefs.

So how do you deal with this?

- **Keep moving** to avoid being anchored to unhelpful relationships. You can't win if you're fighting in-built biases when you could be thriving elsewhere
- **Call time on an unhelpful situation**, but avoid fueling conversations about it. Focus instead on something worthwhile elsewhere, remembering that you get what you focus on. Over time, bad news fizzles as the news treadmill continues to churn out new dopamine and cortisol.

But what if you have to deliver bad news?

The best way to present bad news is to use framing techniques. When you present bad news first, everything that you say thereafter looks like a treat, or upside.

Say for instance, you want a pay rise – you should start *plausibly* high, then work back to what you really want.

Or, if you have your team *regularly* working late, give them a *normal* day and it will feel like a holiday.

It's all a matter of tolerance or context which we saw in the introduction.

If someone lives in adversity, a window of normality feels heaven sent. The opposite works just as well.

Take for instance a corporate performance review or feedback session. My advice is to deliver bad news first, then something positive to end with.

Better still is a shit sandwich – good news, bad news, good news. People remember beginnings and endings much more than they do middles, so the recipient will walk away feeling like *they* snatched some kind of victory from the jaws of defeat. All's well that ends well.

In these examples, you're simply leveraging denial of loss and transforming the loss into something that feels like a gain – however small it may be. It ends like the resolution of a difficult story (which we'll dissect below).

Questions

1. Which elements of your work can become bandwagons

    (platforms for the success of others)? ....

2. Do you need to work more on creativity or marketing? ....

3. How do you deal with bad news? ....

4. When could you hand out shit sandwiches? ....

3. Push Strategies

Strategy #52: Tell Good Stories

People think they want the facts, but more often than not, they prefer a good story.

I had the chance to fire a question at a Hollywood composer, about his incredibly poignant composition for a new movie. I wanted to know just how he had found and eked out the intense emotional heart of the score – expecting an answer about resonance in the movie's ideas. He answered – truthfully and *factually,* trying to be helpful and perhaps a little modest – that he just wrote it in an afternoon and it was done and dusted the following day. No story (from the story teller). Unfortunately, the music never sounded quite as impressive to me again.

It's the ability to construct and tell stories which singularly separates humans from other animals[9]. Everything that we perceive, experience, have, hope for, fear, regret and so on is in the stories we construct in our heads every minute of every day.

A little something about brains: they work – by and large – through prediction. We then knit together information that supports or updates that prediction.

---

[9] Physical abilities aside, story-telling may be a fundamental distinction between humans and other animals. Rich stories originate in our brains' superior ability to combine knowledge from disparate brain regions and this is the fundamental process in creativity.

Why? It's efficient. If we had to make sense of everything in real time our brains would be as big as the moon. But, if there's too little in our lives with no surprise, our brains shrink to a pea. Prediction was efficient in a world where little changed (aka the life of most of our evolution), but safe surprises releases feel good opiates.

Stories are important during change, because they bypass the head and appeal to the heart. Remember we said that dopamine and cortisol are the only reasons we get out of bed (caffeine, nicotine and other drugs aside)?

It's also the case that the heart (read: the subconscious) calls the shots – always.

Plus, our brains are also wired to rapidly pattern-seek[10] and stories are simply patterns that provide a primeval buzz when they confirm our predictions or safely update them (not to forget: keep us alive).

It's not surprising, then, that there's quite a body of evidence to show that impressions (stories) and reactions (choices) are made instantaneously in the subconscious before we are even able to rationalize them consciously.

The rational parts of our brain formed late in our evolution and seem to be supremely good at articulating stories (or patterns) out of events, then

---

[10] Pattern-seeking starts on day one and is fundamental to language acquisition, walking and – well, everything.

provide a narrative coherence which we then communicate to others. It's as if we construct our own reality in real time. When we become aware of events, we first tell the stories to ourselves (internal chatter) to discern patterns of danger, status and coherence, then weave those narratives into something we can tell to others.

This is all for the sole purpose of attracting resource (capital, relationships, co-operation and so on). In other words – we use stories to survive and thrive.

We spend every moment of our lives showing or telling stories of one sort or another to obtain a resource.

Logic and rationality, then, are just ways of explaining in words and communicable structures what the heart already knows and wants. They are, for the most part, utilities for collating and presenting evidence to explain subconsciously made decisions.

So, a question: What makes you unique amongst the sea of office employees the world over? A barrow full of accolades? Nope – everyone can feign a few. Big numbers or dull facts in a presentation? Nope – they're simply not memorable or relatable. Our eyes glaze over with numbers and facts but we can't help but listen to a good story. It's the way to get attention. It's your unique and personal take on the world that counts.

We are wired to engage in and remember a story if it is told well. A well-told story remains vivid inside our heads without any effort or cramming.

Don't believe me? Try this memory hack which turns the ultimate in mundane into a story of sorts:

- Remember a car parking location number or a zip code;
- Then try to remember the same thing as a ridiculously funny image or sequence of images
- Try this for all the parking locations in the car park or zip-codes on your street, making a string of ridiculously amusing images or a story which leads from one item to the next
- You'll find that the more vivid and imaginative the story you construct, the longer you remember it – sometimes being able to recall it even years later.

This works, in part, because the crafting of the story gets your attention for something which would otherwise have been ignored.

Attention, therefore, is the first vital ingredient in story-telling. If *you* want to be impactful and gain the upper hand in negotiations you have to give people stories worth listening to and remembering.

Tell stories in your own unique way. Your own war stories. About your successes and failures. It shows you've been places and done real stuff. You can even tell stories that are not your own because stories that are good enough to tell on are also memorable. They get socialized and repeated and allow others to create conversation.

So, how do you craft stories? Well, remember three things. Show (don't tell), structure and conflict.

But all that comes third. First by a long, long, long shot, you have to have something worth telling. A word mountain – however much agonized over – doesn't make a good story.

Second: understand what *specifically* will deliver the dopamine hit (cathartic moment) that the audience needs without realizing? In a business setting, for example, it could be underdog winning a conflict or competition, or discovering of the key to success. It could it be about reinforcing the power of perseverance, and so on. What specific *hit* is your audience after? Ground zero for delivering that hit is always found in the need for self-validation – perhaps validating a point of view or position, or supporting actions taken. You want your audience think or say: 'I told you so' or 'I knew it' or 'I feel smart'. It's all about the audience.

You could instead induce cortisol to galvanize action through stories of fear or failure or defeat.

The point is, you have to aim for a specific trigger in the heart to land your story.

Story Essentials

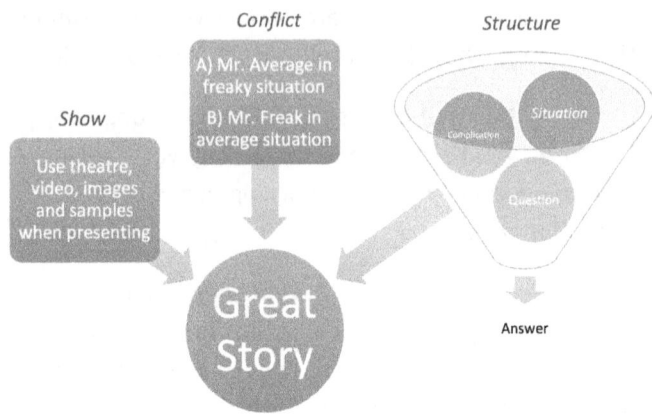

Show, Don't Tell

I can't emphasis this enough if you really want to get through to people.

If you're pitching a product, *show* the product, don't *tell* your audience about it with a PowerPoint.

If you're pitching a solution, *show* evidence of how and where it worked, don't *tell* people that you simply installed it.

Put on theatre by *showing* whenever you're trying to get attention.

You're allowing your story to become that of your audience by showing – that allows them to buy the story. Remember it's all about self-relevance.

Structure

Your favorite stories weren't written, they were built –
word by word – like the house across the road, was
brick by brick, from a template of great stories – just
like all the houses in the row had the same basic
blueprint. To land a good story then, rely on well-
established conventions and repeat them. The best
stories are the ones we want to hear over and over.

And when you've figured out that a story's
worth telling, and way, way, way before you even begin
to think about words, figure out the right delivery
mechanism and requisite structure. A well-crafted
narrative is important for consistent understanding
because it fires similar patterns of meaning in different
individuals with different expectations, whereas a
stream of consciousness isn't going to land, however
compelling your ideas. Plugging in boring facts, figures,
research citations, anecdotes and so on won't engage
an audience already overwhelmed or bored to tears.
Sometimes sound bites or alternative delivery
mechanisms are better suited and may provide the
structure you need. These could include brevity, specific
focus, sound, visuals, timing, and so on.

Luckily, humanity has distilled a story structure
that's resonated with all of human kind since humans
first began and it's likely to work at some level,
whatever delivery approach you use.

Commercial stories, the type that we find
moving, simply follow one simple structure and it's

been re-invented and relabeled over and over in a myriad of ways since the beginning of time. So, trust that it works on other humans!

As Peter Guber puts it in his book _Tell to Win:_ 'challenge, struggle, resolution'.

Start with a mystery, a challenge, or something out of whack, a conflict, a hook, or it's not really a story. There's literally nothing worth writing home about without any of these.

And what's the best hook in the world? What grabs the heart like nothing else? The word _You._ Self-relevance grabs and keeps attention like nothing else. Nothing. In other words, You makes your opening relevant.

Now, try one of these structures to bring your work to life. They all have challenge, struggle, resolution at their heart.

SCQA

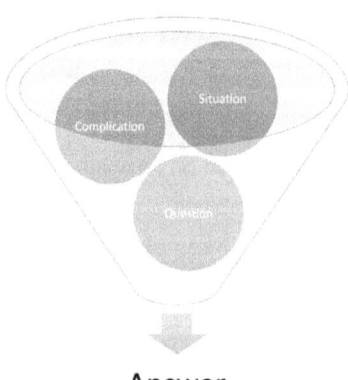

Answer

Use this structure to drive a decision for a new course of action.

1) The **Situation**: This is just basic framing. What's the world like right now? What's happened? The before picture. The status quo. Everything that we know that we know. The prologue or the exposition to open the door and get on the same page. It's how commercial fiction used to begin (now they start with 2, below) – think of Middle Earth. It's the state of tranquility that's about to be shattered by...

2) The **Complication**: This is the challenge to the status quo which grabs attention. Hook - something they care about. Pose a mystery then deepen it e.g. a man in a hole followed by another hole). You're demonstrating that things are not the way they seem. You're convincing an audience that the status quo is doomed. Remember we said visionaries reveal present personal and shared experiences to create connection with the audience in the communication styles above? Think of the wizard turning up in Middle Earth with a world of problems for Frodo Baggins –there's no choice but to change or do something different, which leads to the obvious...

3) **Questions** on everyone's lips. What needs to be done to get back to the status quo? How bad will it be? Provide clues then leave a cliff-hangar to leverage the power of Gestault (your audience will clamor for closure). Can Middle Earth and the world be saved? But remember, this is not the solution – that comes next as...

4) The **Answer,** of course. This is the action which will resolve the complication and restore a status quo. Here, you resolve the mystery and draw lessons, whether cautionary or prescriptive. The world may not be the same as in *the situation* at the beginning, but it will be okay. Frodo *has* to leave and throw the mystical ring in the fire.

This structure works because:

- It follows basic story structure of challenge (complication of the Situation), struggle (coming to terms with the Answer, and what must be done), and subsequent resolution (the awarding of the actual project). Once the journey starts (the project), you simply present this formula over and over and over ad infinitum for new decisions.
- It gets you attention and acknowledgment for the problem before you move everyone up the path toward a resolution.

In the *Situation*, you deliberately start with a picture which is entirely agreeable and non-contentious. In terms of the trust equation, it demonstrates credibility – that you've listened and observed and understood the world as your audience sees it or you've seen something by virtue of experience. The situation is aimed at openness and putting whatever's relevant on the table so that it's a known quantity and that makes it likeable, or at least agreeable.

- As the audience moves up the path and accept each stage, it'll be harder to mentally turn back, as that would mean contradicting the beliefs about the world that they've already accepted.

I would advise you to beware of framing or priming if you're the listener. These essentially pitch the issue in a certain way.

The Situation is where you're most likely to be dangerously framed or primed for a deliberate agenda if you're not thinking. Facts and figures can be plucked out of thin air to present just about any picture any presenter wants.

Unconscious incompetence is often at play here (we talked about that in Volume 2) because a situation analysis is often tarred by a naively narrow spotlight on facts that doesn't take everything into account. There's always something off-stage that's not accounted for – we mistake absence of evidence for evidence of absence. If you read Volume 1, you'll recall the Ladder of Inference in which we tend to ignore what we don't see or understand and find the path of least resistance to a conclusion, especially when we have less information, not more. The ladder says we collate data that supports our agenda avoiding or even rejecting data that opposes it. You need to incorporate diverse outside views to frame a situation effectively.

If you're pitching an agenda, however, remember: a) less is more; and b) like-minded audiences are confirming.

All is Lost Structure

This is ideal for an emotional story, perhaps for change and is the de-facto Hollywood style of story-telling. It's constructed to get attention and designed to be engaging.

A lot like SCQA above, you start with a *Before*, which is followed swiftly by a *Disturbance.* What was life like before, and what threatened that tranquility?

Let's use the movie *The Secret Life Of Walter Mitty* as an example of the archetypal office worker to demonstrate this story structure.

Spoiler alert – stop here and skip this section if you don't want a spoiler for this film – or all Hollywood films – or even any blockbuster novels for that matter. Entertainment may never be the same again once you understand the template.

Life *before* was calm, predictable, orderly and routine for the mailroom guy. He continually fantasized about the adventurous life that he didn't have.

Then, in a *disturbance,* the most important photograph in the company went missing from the mailroom – or did it? Walter might lose his job as a result. That is known as the *hook*. We want to know what happens to this guy. This is Mr. Average thrown into a freaky situation.

Then, precisely 25% on comes the *struggle*, in which he does all manner of weird and wonderful things to try and get the photo back. This is the struggle to overcome the disturbance, in a bid to get back to normality – to get the missing photo. In the process, he becomes a changed man living out the adventures he always fantasized about.

Close to the end – precisely 75% in – comes an *All is Lost* moment. In the Walter Mitty example, this moment comes from finding that the photo was put in the trash by accident – and there's no way to get it back. This is a build-up of story tension.

In the end, he somehow manages to *save the day*, with a surprising resolution. The photo's found and he snatches victory from the jaws of defeat – but is irrevocably changed by his experiences. This is a satisfying resolution.

Personal stories constructed in this way are engaging and memorable. Use a template like this in interviews and social settings like business dinners and so on to give you a personality.

If you can't demonstrate a really poignant personal struggle, your stories will have no personality. They will simply be diaries of averageness.

Five Ws and One H for Gossip or Factual Accounts

This is how news is constructed and police interrogations are conducted.

Who did **What**? **When** and **Where**? **Why** and **How?**

The emotional hook (or challenge) is the *Who did What?* up front. That's usually something unexpected from a well-known personality and it's a shocking revelation that's guaranteed to grab attention.

When and Where? give insight into the struggle of this story.

Why and How? resolve the story with a satisfying explanation.

Conflict

You need to remember that story = conflict. Conflict = story.

Anything else is not a story. It may be a diary or a documentary – perhaps even analysis. But those are not good stories and nor is real life, for the most part – we've edged all conflict out of our daily commute. Offices – if functioning efficiently – run like well-oiled machines and are not normally havens of open, eye-popping conflict.

See how conflict is inherent in the structure above? Conflict gets and maintains our attention. Office life doesn't.

So, how do you create conflict? Use tug of war, irony and paradox.

Think of two simple approaches that represent the sum total of all stories ever told by humanity. In fact, they are simply two ways of telling the *one* story known as The Hero's Journey. Every story is one of these two, but dressed up in one way or another:

A) **Mr. Average finds himself in a freaky situation.** We all want to know how Mr. Average copes with the difficulty of the situation. At work, that could be an annual performance review that went bad or an interesting business trip across the world to somewhere new weird and wonderful. It could be about you saving a business from certain disaster. The bigger the climb for Mr. Average to rise above the freaky situation, the better the story.

B) **Mr. Freak in an average situation.** Yes, the reverse. How does an office full of Mr. Averages cope with a new freak, for instance? Your office might get a new bulldog for a boss, sent in to save underperformance. He kicks butt and fires people. That's a story. The greater the distance between the averageness and freakiness, the more engaging the story.

Okay, so you're wondering what all this means for your quarterly results presentation or the IT department budget. Unfortunately, these are not great story fodder. Remember that business documents, though touted as stories, are not stories per se. They are analytical arguments and dry slabs of fact. Also, PowerPoint and Excel simply weren't built from story DNA.

There are, however, a handful of things that can make a big difference and apply some of the timeless principles of story-telling:

- *Always* decide first whether you're in the business of inducing dopamine or cortisol. It *has to be* one or both – because they are the mechanisms by which humans direct attention and initiate action (besides the promise of nicotine or caffeine!). Dopamine is induced by benefit, and cortisol by loss. Use the former for sustained action or repeat prescription. Use the latter to light a rocket (but just don't expect anyone to come back for more).
- Use images. Words on a slide *tell*, whereas images *show*
- Sprinkle your presentation with two thirds personal experience. Use funny, vivid images and metaphors to bring ideas to life. Here, you're *showing*, not telling
- Use one of the structures outlined above, all of which mimic the basic challenge, struggle and resolution story structure

- Don't confuse presenting (a performance) with putting a written report (analysis) on screen. If you can do it at all, have specifically tailored presentation material. Yes, unfortunately impact does mean a bit of extra work because few of us will go that far!
- Encourage audience interaction to break the monotony of your broadcast. They'll get to share their experience too and weave themselves into the narrative of the presentation. They will, as a result, engage more deeply
- Avoid presenting tables or reams of numbers. Talk to the audience and encourage them to give you several notable numbers which you then write up or transition into place
- Simplicity, consistency and congruence work because these give audiences cognitive ease. They are more likely to avoid thought and challenge and act on your pitch. Talking about consistency, always start with something agreeable so everyone knows which way is up and defenses drop. That could be an articulation of the problem you're trying to solve.
- Whatever you do, don't turn your email into stories. That instead requires the 3-sentence rule – if you can't say it in 3 sentences you need to think about a better way to get your message across. Nonethless, the 3-sentence rule equals story – a beginning, middle and end. Just remember to put the end first for email i.e. what's the resolution you want?

Questions

1. Which story elements are most useful for pitching your work for impact?..

2. How about for social impact with colleagues? ....

Strategy #53: Build Brand Identity and Influence Within your Network

Most of my newer coachees underplay or fail give adequate attention to the single most important success factor in their careers – their network.

Having spent an entire education chasing personal performance accolades, many join the workforce thinking that success is being a solo hero in their own story, delivering the work they do, the best they can, for a boss. That may have been the success strategy fifty or a hundred years back when mobility was significantly limited but that's not the world today. We're all much more connected and power now resides in collaborative networks – not individuals.

Plus, in the *real* world, nothing has value in isolation.

Even a work of art needs a museum and a marketing machine. A world-class singer is nothing without opportunities to perform. A CEO needs opportunities to lead and all of these permissions are granted by others. You'll need others to provide resource and opportunity throughout your career.

Your impact, therefore, is directly proportional to the audience or network you build, particularly with those holding power. You'll understand that bosses are no longer omnipotent or limiting in great careers when you network well.

But go a step further and think of these networks as alliances and partnerships.

What can you and your friends, associates and peers achieve together? That's fundamentally a business.

Many of my coachees tend to overlook the need to nourish peer relationships in particular, tending instead to focus on management relationships and trying to out-compete each other. But the truth is that someday it's their peers who will lead other organizations if they are all heading up the tree together.

A couple of questions to ask yourself:

- What do I bring to a party?
- What do I need others to bring to that party?
- Do I show up consistently?
- What am I about, that my company needs?
- Which roads always lead to me – not just in the company, but in the industry too? Do others know that?
- How can I get the network committed to my success?

- How can I limit access for my rivals to my network? Your network can be one of the most important competitive weapons in your arsenal. We'll talk more about competition in Volume 4.

If nothing else, think of networking as marketing yourself – like marketing any other product or service.

And no-one *can* care about a product or service they even don't know about. You'll have to work at delivering yourself as a service or product to people who matter. People are distracted so the frequency of your marketing effort really matters too. Brand recency stays top of mind whereas distant memories fade quickly.

Try to broker conversations that solve problems so you can get into key organizational conversations and positioned to pick juicy roles before they're advertised.

Be available for those important to you but create some scarcity for those to whom *you* are important. You might enhance your value just through simple demand and supply!

Scarcity is about loss aversion, too – specifically a loss of opportunity or control and can be enhanced by competition for your energy or limited time. People who are rushed, often use scant information to make choices (they are already halfway up their Ladder of Inference[11]) and may – having worked hard to get your attention – vouch for you just to make things easy.

---

[11] Read about the ladder of interference in volume 1

And when people then start talking about you positively you're benefiting from **social proof** which is the most powerful source of credibility in the trust equation. Social proof helps to build a majority and when enough people vouch for you, others will simply follow without thinking.

The upshot is this: stay visible and cultivate support through partnerships and alliances.

You also build influence by doing things for important people and by strategically leveraging the **natural biases** we're all made of. These are described across this entire series.

Look for opportunities to do favors (create connections), or better still to concede (perhaps bend a rule), and the people you help will feel compelled or obliged to **reciprocate** whether or not they consciously chose to.

Start small to create a hook, then build from there – those who reciprocate will feel compelled to behave **consistently** of their own volition thereafter.

Find commonality and create a compelling or common enemy or opportunity. Work on building association.

Remember that, wherever you find two or more people together, you're looking at power centers, each continuously vying for dominance in one domain or another. Corporates and other organizations are no different.

If you can find the power centers and power brokers in your organization, you would do well to align yourself to them.

So, if the ship goes down some day, you're more than likely to be at the top of the right mast and able to keep your head above water. But when the power centers are in ascendancy, you'll be swept up with them anyway.

You can play that game too. You're looking to jump into complimentary relationships, where for instance you – as one party – can on-sell the other, and so on. This can have the competitive effect of deterring rivals from moving into your territory or starving them of opportunity. Look for ways to bundle your skills in a complimentary way, particularly with peers to form a barrier to entry. We'll talk about this again when we look at Competition in Volume 4.

Questions

1. How much of your work time do you allocate to

   networking?..

2. Which tools above could you use to leverage your

   network?..

Strategy #54: Assert Yourself

Feeling a lack of assertiveness is surprisingly common and afflicts everyone at some point. It kills your position in a negotiation.

Let's say you're not getting what you want or need at work or you're unable to speak up in meetings. Perhaps your views aren't considered. You may repeatedly fail to ask for something from a boss or colleague or fail to stand your ground when someone pushes back on your decisions or choices.

Recognize first that a certain amount of not always getting what you want is normal, especially if you're constantly demanding.

Whatever you do, don't confuse the free choice of others to make their own decisions with a lack of assertiveness on your part. An essential element of assertiveness is respecting that others are free to make their own moves, even if you disagree.

There are nevertheless a number of techniques to help you tackle assertiveness. In my experience, it's often a combination of the following.

Assertiveness Cycle

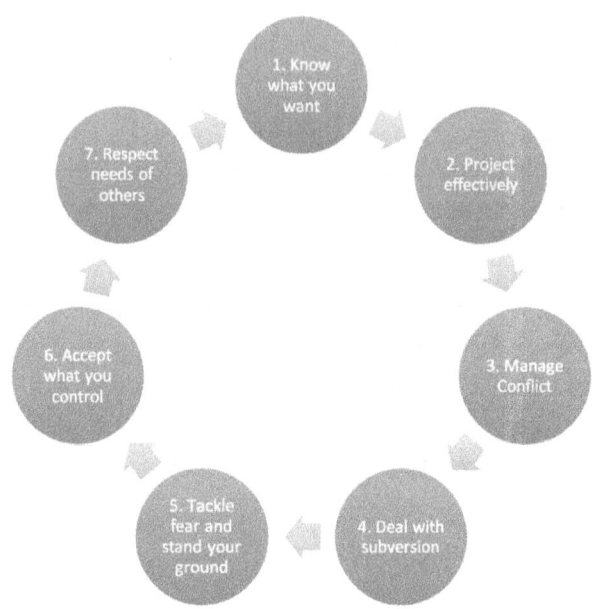

Let's take one at a time.

1) **Clearly knowing what you want** in a given situation *before* it arises sounds obvious, however, knowing what you want isn't always clear. But clearer you can get, the easier it will be to say, ask and even frame or rig the situation in your favor. We'll talk more on framing and rigging in Volume 4 on Competition.

2) **Projecting what you want** in the most effective way. We do this to anticipate and avoid pushback,

and also to say 'No' to what we don't want – but in the right way. We covered pushback and saying 'No' earlier in this book.

3) **Anticipating, expecting and dealing with conflict** effectively. Conflict arises in some shape or form every time you want something that's different to the crowd. Get used to it and learn to expect it if you want to be assertive. When you're good at dealing with conflict the feelings will, in time, diminish, because others – like you – dislike conflict too and will often back down when you hold your ground for just a little bit longer than them. We talked about conflict earlier too.

4) **Recognizing and arming yourself with subversion deflecting techniques**. Others will deliberately subvert you. We'll talk more about tackling subversion in Volume 4 on Competition.

5) **Understand your own *fear* mechanisms** which are wired into your brain. This will help you to stand and fight and *not* flight, but also to calm down quickly after a standoff. You'll find more on this in Volume 1, Self-Awareness, Behavior & Motivation.

6) **Focusing on and making choices about what you control** and recognizing and then letting go of what you don't. You may to choose to attempt to influence what you don't control but it's always a losing battle. Don't walk into that arena.

7) **Understanding and respecting the wants and needs of others** and the choices they are free to make – just like you.

Remember, that assertiveness allows others the same freedom of choice that you have. In TA speak from Volume 1, it's closely associated with Adult-Adult type relationships and with 'I'm Okay – You're Okay' – even though we may differ in our opinions.

It's not about forcing your point of view, throwing your toys out of the pram or steam-rollering over others to get what you want – those behaviors are associated with the *Demanding Parent* and *Rebellious Child* in TA speak. Such demanding behavior can also come from a place of 'I'm Not Okay – You're Okay' (a passive stance), or even 'I'm Okay – You're Not Okay' (an aggressive stance). Read more about these in Volume 1.

Typical Assertive, Passive and Aggressive Behaviors

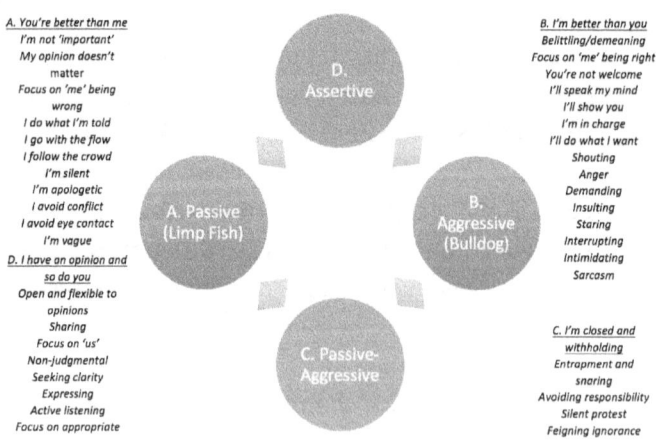

A. You're better than me
I'm not 'important'
My opinion doesn't matter
Focus on 'me' being wrong
I do what I'm told
I go with the flow
I follow the crowd
I'm silent
I'm apologetic
I avoid conflict
I avoid eye contact
I'm vague

D. I have an opinion and so do you
Open and flexible to opinions
Sharing
Focus on 'us'
Non-judgmental
Seeking clarity
Expressing
Active listening
Focus on appropriate

B. I'm better than you
Belittling/demeaning
Focus on 'me' being right
You're not welcome
I'll speak my mind
I'll show you
I'm in charge
I'll do what I want
Shouting
Anger
Demanding
Insulting
Staring
Interrupting
Intimidating
Sarcasm

C. I'm closed and withholding
Entrapment and snaring
Avoiding responsibility
Silent protest
Feigning ignorance

D. Assertive

A. Passive (Limp Fish)

B. Aggressive (Bulldog)

C. Passive-Aggressive

Aggressive simply want to control others, Passives feel like they have no control, Passive-Aggressives want to control others without being obvious (also called deniable aggression).

Though we're not necessarily fixed in one of these passive or aggressive behaviors, we're likely to find one that dominates our personality. Which dominates yours?

Most of us move between positions according to circumstance and more importantly, by virtue of a triggered habitual behavior in our relationships.

Sometimes it's appropriate to be passive, for instance when you don't have a useful point of view or where the stakes are low and you'd rather avoid participation.

Aggressiveness can also be useful when you're threatened and in immediate danger or where there's no time for negotiation. Neither, however, are sustainable as a default mode of behavior all the time.

Perhaps the most interesting position is a variant of aggressiveness, called passive-aggressive. In this mode, individuals deliberately withhold opinions or information in order to prevent others acting effectively or of their own free will. It serves to silently subvert an unwanted course of action and to avoid responsibility for an opinion held or for inaction. It can be associated with Child behavior, in that it's engaged to manipulate situations where someone doesn't have the control they want.

So, if you catch yourself being continuously passive or aggressive, ask yourself if it is the best behavior for the situation. Both of these will lead to a lot of stress and poor relationships if sustained.

If you're normally **passive**:

- Speak up early – about anything. It could simply be small talk around the main conversation. Just learn to get a voice and to allow others to relate to you
- Learn to pitch your ideas effectively. We discussed communication styles above
- Get the information you need to shore up your point of view if you are uncertain
- Prepare for interactions beforehand and understand where you often concede when you shouldn't
- Stop self-deprecation by getting out of your own head and re-directing your energy towards others
- You have a choice like anyone else. At the end of the day, everyone else is simply an employee taking home a paycheck for a contribution just like you, whatever hierarchy the organization might have dreamt up for all of you.
- Resist the temptation to do something just because it's easy. This is a slippery slope and you're walking into your consistency bias which we've talked about.
- Don't be ambushed into accepting something. Practice saying, let's discuss that later, then stand your ground while anticipating incoming pressure. This will eventually recede.

- If you want something, practice just asking. Not a demand – which is bound to fail, but a request. The worst you can get is a no, though don't get yourself into a corner too often (a consistency bias will kick in again). Practice the requiring communication style above.

If you're normally **aggressive**:

- Remember that you can't control what you don't control. End of story. Let go
- Remember that aggressiveness is not sustainable. People will disconnect
- Stop and listen by getting out of your own head and allowing the energy of others to reach you
- Invite input, even if briefly at the start and simply acknowledge the input for what it is without judgment or comparison
- Remember that people can't miss what you didn't say – so don't be so hard on yourself, having not said everything on your mind. It may benefit you to only say what's really useful.

Passive aggressive behavior on the other hand, can be difficult to tackle because it's designed to be hidden.

The best way is to smoke out an offender is by requiring some action and getting public commitment. Because others feel compelled to act consistently with their own motivation, inaction in this situation might then be revealing. This may comprise lateness to meetings or missed deadlines and so on. These can be covert protest or lack of support and may be a good sign that someone's acting on a hidden agenda.

Questions

1. How much of your work time do you allocate to

   networking?..

2. Which of the tools above could you use to leverage your

   network?..

Strategy #55: Impact in Groups

Meetings

Many people find it difficult to make an impact in group settings.

Meetings, for instance, usually have dominant participants that won't allow a word in. Sometimes you just don't fit or you may even genuinely have little to contribute.

The first thing is to reframe your understanding of meetings. Corporate meetings are first and foremost a stage or an arena in which there's an expectation of performance.

These aren't places to try something untested or to get introspective. These are places to display an already polished act. But more than a stage for you, these places are often stages for competing alliances.

So, when you behave as part of a strong alliance in a meeting, you are giving a strong and effective show of power.

Impact is often then handed to you on a plate.

Secondly, when you really have little to contribute, you ought to get out of a meeting if you

can. A lack of contribution becomes self-reinforcing and positions get established surprisingly fast.

You'll get a reputation you'd rather not have.

The third thing is to build support outside and before a meeting for whatever it is that you wish to contribute.

Prepare the ground even down to the environment by starting relevant conversations with one or two participants beforehand, so that you can continue in the same vein inside the meeting room. You'll come across as well connected and your allies will help you win discussions inside the meeting. The point is that you must first have relevance outside of a meeting if you want relevance inside it. Acknowledge new joiners – it's a subtle way to get them on your side through acknowledgment.

Fourth, try to influence meeting agendas beforehand so you can get a speaking part.

Nothing puts you on the map quite like your own stage – so create one.

Fifth, get in early. Say anything – big or small. And speak a little louder (though subtly) to signal you're entering the conversation.

The mere act of participating early lowers yours and everyone else's mental barrier for when you want to chime in later. It's a power play, like draping yourself over the territory.

Say nothing, and it becomes harder for you to get back into the meeting later. First impressions count and once the people around you see you as a mere spectator they will reject impressions to the contrary. The opposite is just as true.

Sixth, try not to go overboard, remembering that it may not be your show.

Respect whoever's show it is, and allow them the stage that they've put up.

Okay, so you're now a meeting pro and pretty soon you'll find yourself having to manage a few, for others who saw better sense and left you to it. Obviously, be organized and efficient, remembering that it's a stage – not just for you, but everyone.

Let others have their say, because, paradoxically, desperately hogging the limelight looks like clamoring, and can reverse your impact. Self-interest becomes evident and that diminishes trust.

Encourage interaction. In terms of energy re-direction, you want to pull energy away from introspection, while limiting flagrant broadcasting by opportunists. Remember, the middle ground is a conversation.

Seventh, sit to the right of the leader.

Your words will enter the right ear and head straight to the left brain which processes language. The words of the right-hand man always resonate louder.

Finally, in groups – do have your antennae ready for being volunteered without your permission?

Savvy managers often dump on others, especially during calls.

When a meeting's going well, with pace, energy and enthusiasm, short-term emotion derails objectivity and you'll be much more likely to be agreeable, even when it's not in your own interests. Publicly made commitments, however dumb in retrospect, stick like glue.

My advice is to avoid making public commitments when volunteered, unless they're already part of your role. Pay particular attention to this if you're normally passive.

Instead, agree to discuss new commitments outside the meeting or call. Remember, you may have a decision or tradeoff to make with whatever else is already on your plate.

If you're leading a meeting, recognise the Operating Modes:

- Expressives need to be focused on doing things, otherwise a lot more will be said than done, when all is said and done
- Creatives may need to be reeled in so their ideas make sense to others in the room
- Analytical or introverted types might be pre-occupied by doing their own thing. Get them off

their laptops and out of their heads and
contributing along with others
- The carers may need to be encouraged to be more
  demanding
- Controllers have to be encouraged to step back and
  allow others to speak up
- Most 'leaders' perpetually push communicate then
  wonder why leadership is such a lonely role. They're
  not connecting with anything beyond their own
  ego.

Presentations

You may have heard it so often that you'd be forgiven
for thinking that Death by PowerPoint was a marketing
slogan of Microsoft's Office software.

Unfortunately, PowerPoint has become an
intractable time hog in business life. The world's most
vaunted modern day CEO, Steve Jobs of Apple, was
even said to have banned presentation slides from
management meetings (not just because it was a rival's
product); and it's not hard to see why. When you add
up the bazillion hours spent fiddling with fonts, color
schemes and lining up boxes – not to mention a roughly
equivalent amount of time bludgeoning others with
slides around tables and in auditoriums – you begin to
realise how big an issue it has become. Unfortunately
for PowerPoint, it has long since become memorable
for the wrong reasons.

Let's remember that presentations are first and foremost a show – a stage.

If you treat presentations like theatre by involving the audience, you'll have a greater impact.

Also, the audience won't miss what they've not seen – so leave stuff out!

In the language of energy re-direction, theater turns a broadcast into a communication. The story you're telling becomes the story of the audience and that's a powerful story. Here are some further tips:

- **Pace yourself,** by giving your audience time to react and interact. Slowing down is a critical leadership communication skill, conveying confidence in what's said. That in turn forces economy with words and makes you keep things simple. Simplicity leads to audience cognitive ease. In contract, speaking fast is like trying to escape your words and close off opportunities for challenge. Others perceive that as a lack of power and presence

- When something is doubtful, **leave it out**. Save it for discussion rather than committing it to paper – or slides

- It can be useful to **throw in a distraction** if you're facing a potentially hostile or vocal audience. In other words, a ruse or a rabbit hole, at which you could pretend to take a pot shot. Disruptive audiences will usually then get their Gestalt for having chimed in and may well leave your main agenda alone

- If you're one of such an audience, however, **doubting, grilling and stupid questions** – in a public forum – are never welcomed. They make a poor show when you're trying to build alliances and impact. They convey self-interest – the inverse of trust. Furthermore, criticising is always much easier than creation.

Conversely, **supporting and encouraging language and solutions** significantly magnifies impact in groups – even when you don't agree with everything that's said.

Remember – *no* **is always accompanied with a** *yes* **to something undeniably better.**

Questions

1. Which of these tactics will most improve your impact in groups? ....

2. Can you ask someone for feedback immediately after group events?..

Closing Remarks

I hope the strategies in this book have given you the tools to do the right things and to do those things right – for big impact.

We've learnt powerful strategies to:

- **Project with power**: #46: Build Rapport and Power with Presence; #47: Work the Charisma Formula
- **Communicate effectively to get what you want, in every situation**: #40: Push and Pull Energy Redirection and Presence; #41: Communicate & Negotiate Purposefully; #43: Defensive Versus Offensive; #51: Deliver bad news in a Shit Sandwich; #54: Assert Yourself; #55: Impact in Groups
- **Story-telling and PR approaches that get people on board with your ideas**: #44: Build Trust; #45 Ask for Help; #48: Master Conflict with a Yes, instead of a No; #50: Create bandwagons; #53: Build Brand Identity and Influence Within Your Network; #52: Tell Good Stories
- **Take others with you**: #42: Tell or Collaborate?; #49: Leaders Help Others Achieve Success.

Okay, now just go and practice these things! Only deliberate practice – and correcting your mistakes – makes perfect.

I hope you've learnt that simply showing up at work and quietly doing the external stuff in your job to the best of your ability is the least of your challenges for creating big impact. Those climbing the ladder will be throwing all of the above – and more – at you, whether or not you are aware of it.

Remember also that learning is doing, not just reading or memorizing. Take one strategy at a time and make it part of your habit or routine. Incorporate another when the previous one's under your belt. Finally, dip back in and find something new on another commute as you progress.

I'm confident that the material will be life changing if you systematically incorporate it into your life, because I've seen that in everyone I've coached.

This series is certain to benefit others, so don't hold back – share the strategies, whether in the office or at home, and help others get on track.

Talk to your boss, mentors, coaches, colleagues, family, or friends, and ask them to help you build an objective picture of *you* – from their perspective.

Please also be sure to review the book – describing how it helped you – on Amazon, iBooks, Kobo, or wherever you purchased it. That helps others to discover it and also provides feedback for future improvements.

Finally, if you want to join a training program based on the content of this book, or if you require coaching, or even if you just want more impact strategies, look for other books in the series at 60strategies.com or follow the links in the front of this book.

Good luck, and let me know how you are doing via the series' website, at 60strategies.com

If you haven't already, go back and discover how to be Self-aware and manage Behavior & Motivation in Volume 1 and Achieve Notable Goals in Volume 2

You're now ready to discover how to Complete & Secure Your Limelight with Volume 4

Get the books @ 60strategies.com